UNITED NATIONS ECONOMIC COMMISSION FOR EUROPE

Supporting Innovative High- Growth Enterprises in Eastern Europe and South Caucasus

UNECE Policy Handbook

UNITED NATIONS
Geneva, 2021

This publication is issued in English only.

United Nations publication issued by the United Nations Economic Commission for Europe.

ECE/CECI/28

UNITED NATIONS PUBLICATION

eISBN: 978-92-1-005809-4

FOREWORD

It is well known that the private sector, especially small and medium-sized enterprises (SMEs), is an essential part of any well-functioning economy. In fact, a small sub-group of these firms play a disproportionately important role in job creation, productivity growth and innovation – in short, in discovering and building the foundational elements for reaching the Sustainable Development Goals (SDGs). These innovative high-growth enterprises (IHGEs) are *transformational entrepreneurs* that lead the way and experiment with new ideas for creating value and tackling sustainable development challenges such as the imperative to ensure sustainable production and consumption (SDG 12), and transitioning towards an increasingly circular economy.

The 2020 UNECE Innovation Policy Outlook, reviews the scope and quality of innovation policies and institutions across the six countries of the Eastern Europe and South Caucasus sub-region (EESC), i.e. Armenia, Azerbaijan, Belarus, Georgia, Moldova and Ukraine, It points out that enabling and nurturing a strong cadre of such entrepreneurs is especially important. These entrepreneurs, by putting innovative ideas into practice, help to diversify and upgrade the EESC economies, unleashing the potential of the knowledge economy and contributing to progress towards the sustainable development goals.

After a painfully rocky first decade following independence, EESC countries have made substantial progress in their transition towards establishing vibrant, inclusive market economies, including improving the legal and regulatory environment and promoting innovation. Today, EESC economies feature a highly educated work force, moderate wage costs, large diaspora populations and increasing access to trade and investment opportunities, a commitment to public research and continued efforts to strengthen their innovation systems. As the analysis of UNECE Innovation Policy Outlook 2020 demonstrated, the future potential is impressive – as some emerging islands of excellence in sectors such as export-oriented information and communication technology (ICT) services show. IHGEs are central to spreading this dynamic more broadly across EESC economies and societies.

Successfully doing so means paying increased attention to the needs, constraints, and incentives that potential innovative entrepreneurs face – many of which differ substantially from those of the private sector at large. This handbook aims to help policymakers understand these factors and explore how support measures could mitigate constraints and, in a targeted way, make sure that more and broader experimentation with ideas takes place in their societies to find out what works and what does not.

The handbook draws on research, consultations and insights gleaned from an on-going capacity building programme for the EESC region that has been made possible through the financial support of the Government of Sweden. It is part of larger UNECE efforts to support EESC economies in increasing their competitiveness and ensuring inclusive growth through innovation. We hope that this handbook will serve as a useful source of guidance and inspiration in the efforts of EESC countries to promote innovation for sustainable development and for a circular economy transition in the decade to come.

Olga Algayerova

Under-Secretary-General of the United Nations

Executive Secretary of the United Nations Economic Commission for Europe

PREFACE

The United Nation Economic Commission for Europe (UNECE) supports EESC[4] countries in promoting innovation and advancing sustainable development. This handbook emerged from a capacity building programme on policies and institutions to enable and support innovative high-growth enterprises (IHGEs) in the EESC sub-region. The work is overseen by the UNECE Committee on Innovation, Competitiveness and Public-Private Partnerships.

As a first step, supported by the Swedish Government, the UNECE and the OECD organized a dedicated workshop in Minsk, Belarus in March 2019 to outline the key concepts on IHGEs and discuss financing of innovative firms.

Secondly, in July-August 2020 a series of fact-finding interviews were conducted with stakeholders from the six countries to identify the drivers and barriers for IHGEs and provide insight on the state of play of policy measures relevant for IHGEs in the EESC sub-region.

Figure 0.1 • Developing the handbook

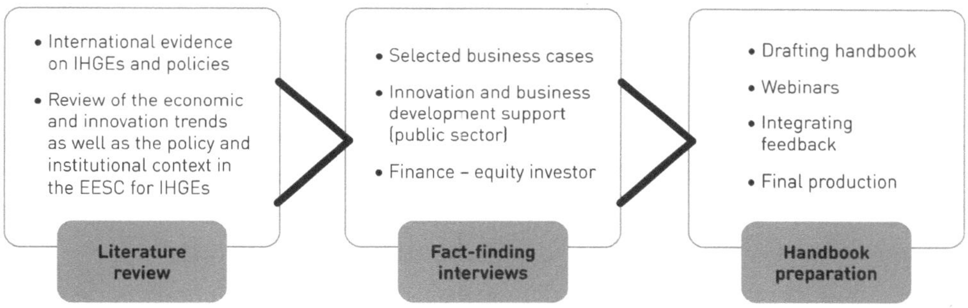

Source: UNECE

Thirdly, two webinars on policies for IHGE policy were organized in September 2020[5], bringing together stakeholders from the six EESC countries and experts from more advanced economies to discuss: i) effective state support services and regulatory frameworks for IHGEs, and ii) enhancing IHGEs access to finance.

The handbook seeks to support policymakers in the EESC sub-region to design effective policies and institutions to further enable and foster the potential of innovative, high-growth entrepreneurship as invaluable drivers for innovation-led sustainable development[1]. High-growth innovative firms have a key role in jobs and value creation as they experiment with new ideas and respond to new incentives (e.g. technological and regulatory changes as well as global market and consumer trends while also contributing to structural economic change through the creation of new markets and better domestic integration into the global economy. IHGEs could thus help EESC countries not only to drive their needed economic transformation but also to achieve sustainable development[6] while addressing the novel social and economic challenges created by the COVID-19 pandemic.

ACKNOWLEDGEMENTS

The handbook was developed within the framework of the UNECE project "Promoting innovation policy capacities in Eastern Europe and the Caucasus" implemented with the financial support of the Government of Sweden through the Swedish International Development Cooperation Agency (SIDA). The project aims to support the governments of the six EESC countries in promoting innovation and competitiveness while ensuring the sustainable economic development of the sub-region, including by means of fostering innovative high-growth entrepreneurship as an important lever for structural transformation.

This publication was produced under the leadership of Elisabeth Tuerk, Director of the UNECE Economic Cooperation and Trade Division and under the overall supervision and guidance of and contributions from Anders Jönsson, Chief of the UNECE Innovative Policies Development Section. The main author of the publication was Alasdair Reid, Policy Director of the European Future Innovation Systems Centre, Belgium. The publication benefited from contributions from Katia Adamo, Economic Affairs Officer at the UNECE Innovative Policies Development Section and Lyudmyla Tautiyeva, a consultant with the UNECE Innovative Policies Development Section. Lyudmyla Tautiyeva coordinated the project while Ludmila Boichuk provided administrative assistance.

The continuous engagement of the national partners in each of the six countries, i.e. the Ministry of High-Tech Industry of Armenia, the Ministry of Transport, Communications and High Technologies of Azerbaijan, the Belarusian Institute of System Analysis and Information Support for the Scientific and Technical Sphere (BELISA), Georgia's Innovation and Technology Agency (GITA), the Ministry of Education, Culture and Research of Moldova and, finally, the National Academy of Sciences of Ukraine, has been essential throughout the project. Special appreciation is due to the representatives of the public and private sector from the EESC region for sharing their invaluable experiences through a range of interviews[1]. The authors would also like to thank all the participants of the capacity-building webinars in March 2019 and September 2020 for their valuable insights and contributions.

Several experts and organizations reviewed and commented on the findings and recommendations, including Ariel Ivanier, UN RCO in Belarus; Dimo Calovski, UNCTAD; Fernando Santiago Rodriguez, UNIDO; Francesco Alfonso, OECD; Mika Juha Vepsalainen, UNECE; national government and civil society representatives from the six EESC countries, in particular Radzivon Marozau, BEROC[2], Belarus, and Yevhen Anhel, IER[3], Ukraine.

Ian Silver edited and Marie-Christine De Sa created the graphic design for the publication.

CONTENTS

LIST OF TABLES

Part I: IHGEs as drivers of economic growth and sustainable development in the EESC sub-region

Part 2: Policies to promote IHGEs

Part 3: A roadmap for boosting the potential of IHGEs in the EESC

Annexes

LIST OF FIGURES

Part 3: A roadmap for boosting the potential of IHGEs in the EESC

LIST OF BOXES

Part I: IHGEs as drivers of economic growth and sustainable development in the EESC sub-region

Part 2: Policies to promote IHGEs

Part 3: A roadmap for boosting the potential of IHGEs in the EESC

Annexes

LIST OF ABBREVIATIONS

AI	Artificial Intelligence
AM	Account manager
BDS	Business development service
BELISA	Belarusian Institute of System Analysis and Information Support for Scientific and Technical Sphere
BPO	Business process outsourcing
CIT	Corporate income tax
CRW	Company Review Workbook
EAEU	Eurasian Economic Union
EBAN	European Business Angel Network
EBRD	European Bank for Reconstruction and Development
ECSP	European Crowdfunding Service Providers
EESC	Eastern Europe and South Caucasus
EIF	European Investment Fund
ENIF	Enterprise Innovation Fund
ERP	Enterprise resource planning
EU	European Union
GAP	Growth Advantage Programme
GBP	British pound sterling
GDP	Gross domestic product
GFIN	Global Financial Innovation Network
GITA	Georgia's Innovation and Technology Agency
HTP	High Technologies Park
ICT	Information and communication technology
IFIs	International Financial Institutions
IHGE	Innovative high-growth enterprise
IÖB	Innovation-promoting public procurement platform in Austria
IP	Intellectual property
KPIs	Key performance indicators
OECD	Organisation for Economic Co-operation and Development

PCP	Pre-Commercial Procurement
PPI	Public Procurement of Innovation
R&D	Research and development
R&I	Research and innovation
SDG	Sustainable development goal
SE	Scottish Enterprise
SIDA	Swedish International Development Cooperation Agency
SMEs	Small and medium-sized enterprises
STAN	Science and Technology Angels Network
STEM	Science, technology, engineering and mathematics
UNECE	United Nations Economic Commission for Europe
US	United States of America
UVCA	Ukrainian Venture Capital and Private Equity Association
VC	Venture capital/capitalist
WB EDIF	Western Balkans Enterprise Development & Innovation Facility
ZCFI	Zubr Capital Fund

EXECUTIVE SUMMARY

This UNECE handbook aims to support policymakers in Eastern Europe and the South Caucasus sub-region to design effective policies that optimize the potential for innovative, high-growth entrepreneurship. The six countries are in transition to a knowledge-based economy, a transition which requires important structural transformation and the identification of key drivers to make this happen. Innovative high-growth enterprises (IHGEs), due to their potential in driving job growth and value creation as they experiment with new ideas and respond to new incentives (e.g. technological, regulatory and market trends), can become one of the driving factors of this transformation. **Through experimentation with the new ideas, IHGEs can contribute to the needed structural economic changes, create new market niches and positive societal spill-overs** (e.g. meeting societal challenges).

The economies of the EESC sub-region are at a turning point. After several decades of reforms, the baseline conditions for"doing business"have improved and governments have put in place policies and institutions that meaningfully support private sector development. Nevertheless, EESC economies suffer from low productivity and while services have become the backbone of the economy in several countries, a significant share of the service sector is domestically orientated, has lower capital and skills intensity and hence is less productive than export-oriented industries. This makes **diversifying and upgrading both manufacturing and services, especially those with export potential, a strategic imperative – a process in which IHGEs can play an essential role**.

A common misconception is the implicit association that innovation is restricted to high-technology start-ups or to commercializing the results of cutting-edge scientific research. In fact, the greatest potential for IHGEs in EESC economies resides in their ability to absorb ideas that have proven their value abroad or in different contexts – from business models (e.g. creating and experimenting with business models based on digital platforms), organizational models and business process engineering while translating new ideas into practice in established sectors (e.g. energy, health care, or agriculture). Many impressive examples of high growth can be found in sectors such as construction, nursing homes and horticulture. While it is important to enable and support growth as well as diversification among recent success stories, such as ICT service exports, effective IHGE policies should be able able to facilitate the realization of potential across society – often in unexpected areas. In other words, **IHGE policies should not target specific sectors or technologies but rather activities with specific features, such as novel ideas with substantial potential spill-over effects on the rest of the economy.** While many innovative initiatives fail, those that succeed create enormous social value, including triggering the emergence of entirely new sectors of activity.

Target groups include:

1. Start-ups with the ambition to scale;
2. Established manufacturing or service firms planning growth through upgrading or diversifying products, organizational innovation, or new business models;

3. Spin-offs from large firms;
4. Attraction of ambitious entrepreneurs and/or scalable companies from abroad to invest in local operations, especially in potentially tradeable sectors;
5. Research-based spin-offs emerging from the public or private higher education sector.

The extent to which each of these routes are realistic for each EESC country varies, but the above remains broadly reflective of the current potential of applying each route throughout the EESC sub-region. The main policy effort across the region so far has been *focused on building "start-up ecosystems"* generally in the ICT field and more specifically in digital services and software but with some "hardware" elements linked to the Internet of Things, AI (artificial intelligence) and the like. A lot of effort by both public agencies and private stakeholders to foster start-up communities has been made. However, instruments such as incubators, accelerators as well as technology and science parks remain unevenly developed and often lack effectiveness, with more focus placed on the start-up phase rather than on later scale-up phases that are crucial for the success of innovative ventures.

Given the uncertain and fast-moving nature of innovation, many of the typical constraints that the private sector faces in the EESC sub-region apply to an even greater extent to IHGEs – compounding the already high risk inherent to innovation. Dealing with higher risks, regulatory obstacles (e.g. product standards) and the lack of the right skills are particularly daunting, preventing much innovation from taking place given the inordinate risks the would-be entrepreneur and investor face. In consequence, the sustained development of IHGEs relies on a set of interdependent factors that are not only related to the capacities that need to be built at the individual firm level but also depend on creating favourable macro-framework conditions for high growth.

IHGEs are inherently different from most SMEs and, as such, broad SME policies are inadequate to successfully meet specific IHGE needs. In this regard, policy intervention should be directed both at enhancing an enabling environment for innovative activity and the development of targeted IHGEs initiatives to support innovative firm's growth that would not happen otherwise. Incentives and exemption (e.g. corporate income tax) schemes commonly employed around the globe are often better adapted to existing firms operating in well-established sectors. IHGEs in EESC countries, on the other hand, worry not only about the substantial risk involved in any innovation, but about a range of fundamental concerns that such incentives do not mitigate, such as regulatory risk, access to specialised expertise, and raising external risk-friendly external capital to help develop and market novel products and services.

Alongside overarching structural reforms, targeted support to IHGEs requires asking the right questions, such as who to support, with what policy, and how such support should be provided - are all essential considerations. Policymakers should consider the importance of analysing "trigger points" to help identify potential IHGEs before they start growing; addressing barriers to growth at each step of a firm's development and finding the right tools for support. In this respect a government needs to play a "coordinator" role, enhancing links between the potential IHGEs and the critical resources for their growth, such as being able to scale-up expertise, hire talented employees and access growth capital.

Of particular importance to target and justify public support are market validation and potential positive spill-over effects. Thus, the relevant question for a policymaker becomes not "which are the high-growth firms in my economy", but rather "which are the firms with high-growth potential that do not grow because of the existence of market or system failures that policy could seek to correct".

Although IHGEs are typically a sub-set of SMEs, their needs are inherently different; targeted advice and a bespoke support programme drawing from a toolbox of services is thus required. The policy toolbox proposed in this handbook is structured into five main types of public sector intervention. These policy tools have worked elsewhere (e.g. the Nordic countries, the Baltic states, Belgium, France, Ireland, Singapore and the UK) and can be adapted to the EESC countries. They include:

1. **Measures to foster a pro-growth business environment** (a regulatory framework conducive to innovation and growth; taxation to incentivize R&D and investors; demand side measures with the Government acting as a first mover in purchasing innovative products or services);
2. Delivery of tailored services to IHGEs packages (high growth programmes based on a client management approach; developing ecosystems and peer-to-peer networks; access to innovation services and infrastructure);
3. **Access to finance adapted to each growth stage** (grant and loan instruments; crowdfunding, business angel investors and accelerators; venture capital: co-investment and fund of funds models);
4. **Reinforcement of the internal capabilities of the firm to grow** (leadership skills, availability of employees with the necessary technical and creative skills, talent attraction and retention);
5. **Internationalization and business-to-business networks** (advice on market trends and entry; international networks, including diaspora links).

Such a targeted approach requires a dedicated team with the skills, flexibility, and incentives to scout for potential IHGEs based on clear criteria and deliver support likely to ensure that more experimentation with strong potential social return takes place than otherwise would be the case. **This involves an account management scheme that could be introduced gradually** – with account managers engaging with potential clients, diagnosing their needs, evaluating the rationale and potential for support while also putting together a comprehensive, tailored package drawing largely from support measures already in place.

Regional cooperation through **a broader regional initiative could lead the way**. An EESC IHGE facility could comprise a fund of funds and a support hub. The fund of funds would provide a mechanism for investing both in national co-investment funds (with business angels or VC investors) with a focus on supporting companies that would seek to expand regionally in the EESC sub-region and globally. The support hub would provide expertise to adjust legal frameworks for investment, as a pre-condition for improving access to equity finance and advisory services to national SME agencies and related bodies on moving to a portfolio (client management) approach to support IHGEs or set up pilot IHGE programmes.

A READERS' GUIDE TO THE HANDBOOK

This handbook seeks to inspire policymakers and stakeholders working to foster innovative high-growth enterprises (IHGEs). It is structured to be read both as a coherent text from beginning to end but also provides detailed insight in discrete sections that can serve as a reference when working on designing and reforming policies and institutions to enable and incentivize innovative initiatives in the private sector.

After introducing the central concepts (Part 1), this handbook explores the rationale for public support (Part 2.1) and proposes a toolkit of measures, institutions and processes for to effectively support IHGEs (Part 2.2). The final part proposes a roadmap for rolling out such support in the Eastern Europe and South Caucasus sub-region (Part 3.1) as well as avenues for cooperation among the six EESC countries (Part 3.2).

Figure 0.2 • Structure of the Handbook

Part I

- Shifting to innovation-led development: the challenge for the EESC sub-region
- Innovation and high-growth enterprises – drivers of economic transformation
- Innovative high-growth enterprises in the EESC sub-region – state of play

Part II

The rationale for policy intervention: why IHGEs need targeted polices

- Why (should Government support IHGEs)
- Who (which firms)
- What (sort of support)
- How (channels can deliver the support)

A policy toolkit to foster IHGEs

- Measures to foster a pro-growth business environment
- Business development services for IHGEs
- Finance and investment services adapted to growth stages
- Reinforcing firms' in-house capabilities to grow: skills and talent
- Going global: networking and scaling in international markets

Part III

A roadmap for boosting the potential of IHGEs in EESC

Designing and implementing a policy for IGHEs

Cross-cutting recommendations: an EESC sub-region business scale-up initiative

Source: UNECE

Throughout the handbook, we point readers interested in more details to additional sources (publications, websites, etc.) and illustrate central points with case studies and examples.

Notes

1 A full list of interviewees can be found in the Annexes.

2 BEROC Economic Research Centre at http://www.beroc.by/en/

3 IER Institute for Economic Research and Policy Consulting at http://www.ier.com.ua/en

4 Armenia, Azerbaijan, Belarus, Georgia, Moldova, Ukraine

5 See: https://www.unece.org/cicppp/cecimeetings/icp/events/2020/webinar-promoting-support-policies-for-innovative-high-growth-enterprises-in-eastern-europe-and-the-caucasus/doc.html The presentations made are available for download.

6 https://www.un.org/sustainabledevelopment/development-agenda/

Part I

IHGES AS DRIVERS OF ECONOMIC GROWTH AND SUSTAINABLE DEVELOPMENT IN THE EESC SUB-REGION

1.1 Shifting to innovation led development: the challenge for the EESC sub-region

More than three decades after independence, the six EESC countries continue their transition towards market and knowledge-based economies. Grouped together by their middle-income status and their geographical location, the countries are somewhat dissimilar in size (territory and population) and income per capita but face similar policy challenges, albeit to varying degrees. A spate of ambitious reforms enabled strong growth in the first decade of this century, driven by the accumulation of capital (machinery, etc.), attractive investment opportunities and rising consumer spending, with the latter arising from growing debt, remittances and wages on the supply side. All these factors, however, are waning and growth is slowing throughout the entire sub-region.

The EESC economies suffer from low productivity against a backdrop of "de-industrialization" with manufacturing and service businesses struggling to automate and upgrade technologically. Although services have become the backbone of most EESC economies, most services are domestically oriented, have lower capital and skills intensity and are less productive than the remaining industrial (including construction) sectors. Compared with Central Europe and the Baltics, productivity in the services sector is significantly lower in all six EESC countries. Sectoral services-led growth is driven mainly by the financial sector, transport and public services rather than by export-oriented high value added, knowledge-intensive services, as in Western European countries (UNECE, 2020). This makes diversifying and upgrading manufacturing and shifting towards **knowledge intensive** services, especially those with export potential, a strategic imperative across the sub-region.

The emergence of IHGEs helps a national economy reposition towards **innovative products and services** designed, produced and then exported on international markets. The growth of innovative firms can help the shift towards higher value-added production that generates higher living standards. For a business with growth ambitions, the first factor influencing the potential to grow is the scale of the home market (population, average income) and the relative sophistication of consumer demand for more innovative value-added products or services. In the EESC sub-region, Ukraine has the largest national market, however, income per head and the geopolitical situation mean that for innovative Ukrainian start-ups the home market advantage is limited. As such, **'going global' by expanding rapidly out of the home market is a necessity for innovative firms located anywhere in the EESC sub-region.**

Yet, there has only been a limited shift in the sub-region towards exporting **more complex** products or services to global markets[1]. A positive development has been the emergence of export-oriented **information and communication technology (ICT) as well as business process outsourcing (BPO) services** across the region, especially in Belarus and Armenia, drawing on growing demand, good skill levels in mathematics and software engineering and competitive wages. However, the (World Bank, 2019) concluded that "*while a vibrant ICT industry is rapidly emerging in Ukraine, constituent firms are primarily focused on relatively low-value-added outsourcing within the ICT global value chain*". In Armenia, opportunities for upgrading may come through closer integration of advanced ICT services (World Bank, 2020) with engineering businesses. Similarly, there is potential for higher growth in 'traditional' manufacturing by improved supply chain linkages with international retailers, e.g. food producers in Moldova (OECD, 2020). Hence, governments should **ensure synergies between support for IHGE and measures to help existing or emerging sector position in higher value-added segments of global markets**.

1.2 Innovation and high-growth enterprises – drivers of economic transformation

This handbook examines the policy tools available to support the emergence and development of IHGEs. There are various definitions used for statistical purposes (Annexes) of a high-growth enterprise based on the growth of the number of jobs created or their turnover. However, in the handbook, the focus is not on high growth per se, but on the transformational effect of enterprises that innovate to grow. Hence, the handbook defines **IHGEs** as firms that:

- Have at least 10 employees at the beginning of their growth;
- Have average annualized growth in number of employees and/or turnover greater than 10 per cent per annum over a three-year period;
- Engage in innovation, defined in a broad sense as any activity that involves new or significantly improved products or business processes, business models, etc.

Rather than describing the firms to be supported, this definition should be used to track the success of a policy intervention by monitoring the number of small and medium sized enterprise (SMEs) that fall into this category of IHGEs after a policy intervention.

IHGE policies are complementary to broad private sector development and entrepreneurship and start-up policies. While IHGEs are a subset of SMEs in an economy, most micro- and small

Box 1.2 The focus of attention – IHGEs

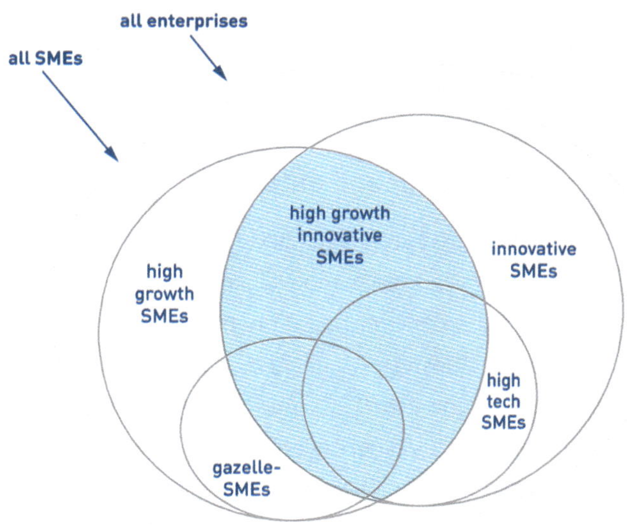

Source: UNECE, adapted from (Lilischkis, 2011).

Note: Circles sizes do not reflect the actually existing number of companies. In particular, high-growth enterprises and innovative enterprises are in reality just a small share of all enterprises. Not shown: There are gazelles that are not SMEs.

enterprises do not grow or engage in innovation. For instance, the propensity to innovate or to seek out opportunities to scale-up will vary depending on the share of SMEs in an economy that are necessity-driven[1] rather than opportunity-driven[2]. Moreover, on average, SMEs are less productive, innovative and export-oriented (European Commission, 2019) than the total population of firms. Indeed, the average SME generates more limited spill-overs of technology and managerial know-how into the economy compared to IHGEs (OECD, 2018). In the EESC sub-region, SMEs represent up to 99% of all enterprises and account for around half of total private sector employment. However, they are less innovative and less productive than the economy on average, for instance, SMEs generate around 47% of total value added and are more concentrated in low value-added sectors, such as the wholesale and retail trade in the EESC region (OECD, 2020).

The potential sources for innovation driven growth are broad and varied...

To support effectively the emergence of IHGEs in the EESC sub-region, policymakers should adopt a broad view of innovation, going beyond a focus on high-tech start-ups, scientific outcomes and intellectual property (IP) rights. In fact, most innovative potential lies in absorbing and adopting ideas that have proven their worth elsewhere, either abroad or domestically but in different economic sectors. IHGE policies should aim to enable and encourage entrepreneurs to implement a wide range of ideas and come up with solutions to challenges at both the national and global levels. The dominant innovation process is likely to be through the so-called 'doing-using-interacting' mode, with enterprises learning by exporting and participating in global value chains. This can also occur through IT outsourcing companies that spawn start-ups based on ideas from outsourcing contracts. Experimenting with ideas may lead to innovation in sectors that are often perceived as not particularly innovative, such as childcare, construction and light industry. This process is at the core of the rationale behind state support for innovation, i.e. while it is hard to predict in which sector innovation will happen, establishing an enabling environment for innovation through effective government policies and institutions increases its probability of happening.

... while a limited subset of SMEs account for most net growth in employment and output...

Over the last two decades (OECD, 2010)[3], research conducted in industrialized, emerging and developing countries has shown that a small number of firms out of the total population of SMEs are high-growth enterprises (3-6 per cent based on employment and 8-12 per cent based on turnover growth). (Grover Goswami & Olafsen, 2019) found that high-growth enterprises in emerging economies account for 8-22 per cent of all firms in the manufacturing and service sectors but create between 50-65 per cent of new jobs (6 per cent to 15 per cent of net new jobs) and between 50-80 per cent of all new sales (gross) in these sectors.

An even smaller group of firms (1 per cent in terms of employment and 2 per cent in terms of turnover) are classified as "gazelles"[4], these are high growth enterprises that are up to five years old. Hence, high-growth enterprises are not necessarily young (start-up) firms, nor are they only found in high-tech fields. Rather, they can and do exist across various economic sectors with this sectoral distribution varying from country to country (Flachenecker F., 2020).

Box 1.1 What is innovation

An innovation is any new or improved product or process (or a combination thereof) that differs significantly from the previous versions of such products or processes and that has been made available to potential users (product) or brought into use by the innovator (an enterprise or any other type of organization). A product innovation is a new or improved good or service while business process innovations concern improvements to the different functions of a firm, such as those involving production, distribution/logistics, marketing and sales, ICT systems, management and business product as well as process development (OECD, EUROSTAT, 2018).

Another way of thinking about innovation is to frame it using the 4Ps model. Innovation can be thought about in terms of four directions of change:

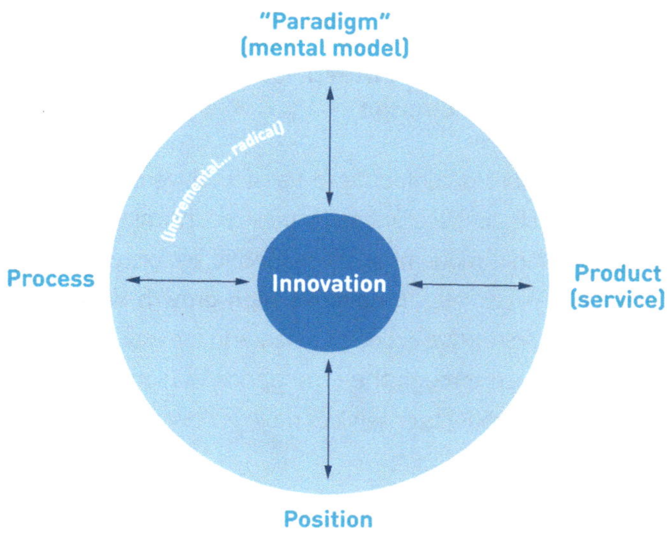

Production innovation: changes in the outputs (products or services) which organizations can offer.

Process innovation – changes in the way in which such outputs are created and delivered.

Position innovation – changes in the context in which products or services are introduced.

Paradigm Innovation – changes in the underlying mental (business) models which frame what an organization does.

Within any of these dimensions, innovations can be positioned on a spectrum from incremental – doing better what is already being done – through to radical – doing something completely different. They can be stand-alone innovations, be part of a system or provide a platform for related innovations (Tidd, 2005).

Source: UNECE, based on (OECD, EUROSTAT, 2018), (Tidd, 2005).

... their high growth is episodic and the trigger points are difficult to anticipate...

Excluding growth through mergers and acquisitions, a firm grows when it exploits a new technological, market opportunity or adopts new business models, operational structures or production methods. (Brown & Mawson, 2013) refer to these important events as **trigger points** which can comprehensively reconfigure a company, providing the catalyst for a business to undertake a period of rapid, transformative growth.

These **bursts of rapid growth** are typically **temporary and episodic.** Firms' growth trajectories normally combine periods of expansion with periods of stagnation or even decline. Indeed, high growth is something that relatively few firms experience and those who do may be "one-hit wonders" (Grover Goswami & Olafsen, 2019).

...so rather than "picking winners" policy should focus on a conducive environment for growth

Given the episodic nature of growth and the variety of possible trigger-points, public policy should not focus on trying to identify and support firms that may be about to enter a period of high growth and then measuring only the direct effects (e.g. employment creation) for these few firms. It is important for policy not to focus on "picking winners" but rather to **develop a conducive 'business ecosystem'** in which firms with significant growth potential and ambitions are able and encouraged to innovate and scale-up their activities. Evidence suggests that an economy with a larger share of high-growth enterprises is associated with greater future economic growth and that there is a positive relationship between productivity growth in an economy and the dynamism of firms' growth rates (Monteiro, 2019). It is **these positive indirect effects of** high-growth enterprises on the economy, so-called spill-overs (e.g. the impact on local suppliers, creation of a positive 'buzz' that attracts more companies and people to locate to a particular area, etc.), that are often overlooked by SME policies.

...and focus on innovative high-growth enterprises that drive broader transformative change

Moreover, not all high-growth enterprises contribute to transformative economic change as their rate of growth may be due to peculiarities in their economic development (e.g. fast growth may indicate the rapid modernization of specific sectors or be driven by short-term spikes in commodity prices, etc.). **Innovative high-growth enterprises** not only grow rapidly but foster positive disruptive economic change in the way that businesses produce and market a product or service, through the emergence of higher value activities and networks or new ways of making products or services more accessible to more people[5]. The case of Vinted is an example.

IHGEs have the potential to be an important element of growth and sustainable development for the EESC economies. Comparing European countries with high R&D expenditure relative to GDP (such as Germany, Slovenia, the Czech Republic) to those with a lower share (such as Slovakia, Lithuania or Cyprus), (Segarra-Blasco, Teruel, & Jové-Llopis, 2018) observed that in the former group, the IHGEs presence is more often driven by R&D and innovation. In the second, IHGEs are driven, on average, more by **business opportunities** building on absorbing and adapting ideas that have proven their worth elsewhere. As discussed in section 1.3, most potential for IHGEs in the EESC sub-region is this second group, based on new business models (e.g. businesses based on digital platforms), business process innovation, as well as growth through new ideas applied to established sectors (e.g. energy, health care, or agriculture).

Several horizontal constraints hit potential IHGEs particularly hard (Calvino, 2016)

Given the uncertain and fast-moving nature of innovation, many of the typical constraints that the private sector in general faces in the EESC sub-region apply to an even greater extent to IHGEs, some of which are detailed below.

1. **Dealing with higher risks,** e.g. commercial risks, knowledge and co-ordination externalities often deter entrepreneurs from exploiting the potential opportunities for innovative high-growth enterprises, especially in less advanced countries where these risks may be higher given issues such as weak financial intermediation, competition policy and bankruptcy regimes. (Calvino, 2016)[6] identified that institutional failures and ineffective regulations (bankruptcy, contract enforcement, civil justice efficiency and those influencing access to finance) are greater obstacles for young high-growth firms.

Box 1.3 How innovative entrepreneurship can support environmental sustainability: the Vinted platform for fashion sharing

Vinted was founded in 2008 in Vilnius, Lithuania, and offers a social marketplace (peer-to-peer platform) for users to sell, buy and swap second-hand clothing. Vinted began when co-founder Milda Mitkute was moving house and realized just how many unworn clothes she had, leading the co-founder, Justas Janauskas, to create a website to trade her clothes to her friends. In the past 12 years, Vinted has grown to operate in 11 European countries grown to become Lithuania's first tech unicorn[a]. In 2019, Vinted announced that its latest funding round had raised €128 million, valuing the company at more than €1 billion (US$1.1 billion). These funds will be used to boost the company's product development and maintain rapid growth across Europe. The company is growing rapidly as the fashion industry comes under growing scrutiny for fuelling a throwaway culture reflecting the increasing concerns of many millennials about the impact of 'fast fashion'. According to Vinted nearly €1.3 billion worth of reused clothing changed hands on its platform in 2019.

Vinted's unicorn status has created positive spill-over effects in the Lithuanian innovation system which has, for example, developed the fastest Fintech licensing process in Europe and five regulatory sandboxes[b]: three in Fintech, one in energy and one Proptecc sandbox.

Source: UNECE, based on https://www.eu-startups.com and https://ww.fashionnetwork.com/news/Green-is-in-fashion-as-vinted-joins-1-billion-club,1163086.html

[a] A unicorn is a term used in the venture capital industry to describe a privately held start-up company with a value of over US$1 billion.

[b] See https://www.eu-startups.com/2019/11/lithuania-crowns-its-first-tech-unicorn-vinted-second-hand-fashion-marketplace-pockets-e128-million-and-secures-e1-billion-valuation/ Regulatory sandboxes enable a direct testing environment for innovative products, services or business models, pursuant to a specific testing plan which usually includes some degree of regulatory lenience combined with certain safeguards.

[c] The application of information technology and platform economics to real estate markets.

2. **Regulatory factors** can have a disproportionately large effect on IHGEs in that the business models or innovative products and services being developed may be running ahead of existing legislation or regulatory frameworks. For example, a European wide study (European Commission, 2019) found that sufficiently flexible labour market legislation is critical to enable rapid scaling up and reduce the downside risks of operations[7]. Moreover, regulations tend to reflect the established technological and business paradigms, which may create barriers to the entry or growth of new disruptive innovations to markets. Targeted improvements to the regulatory environment, while not undermining relevant employment (e.g. avoiding a shift to a 'gig economy') or environmental standards, can have significant impacts on growth prospects in fields such as ICT, business services and firms involved in technology intensive activities (OECD, 2016).
3. **Scarcity of the right skills** hampers experimentation with new products and processes and growth of innovative firms. A survey of 580 IHGEs[8] (European Commission, 2015) underlined that having a good business environment is not sufficient. IHGEs need improved innovation-related capacities via skills development and IP protection. In the long term, greater investment in vocational training and higher education, notably in science, technology, engineering and mathematics (STEM) graduates as well as relevant 'soft skills'[9] is required. In the shorter-term, targeted education and training initiatives as well as encouraging mobility (attracting talent from abroad or helping people who have gone abroad to study to return) can help fill skills gaps (e.g. in key ICT fields or soft skills such as communication and problem solving).

4. **Non-adapted incentives:** many direct (grants, subsidised loans, etc.) and indirect (tax credits) incentives provided by governments may be relevant for standard SMEs but do not fit the needs of IHGEs. For example, investment grants can be important to encourage existing SMEs upgrade production processes, whereas IHGEs are likely to require a more complex mix of financial (grants, equity) and non-financial support (advice and mentoring) to design, develop and test new products or services. Similarly, tax exemptions granted to specific (e.g. 'high-tech') sectors of an economy may fail to reach potential IHGEs in other existing or emerging sectors.

As a consequence, **the sustained development of IHGEs relies on a set of interdependent factors that are not only related to the capacities that need to be built at the individual firm level but also depend on creating favourable framework conditions at the macro level to promote high growth.**

Figure 1.1 · Framework conditions for innovative high-growth enterprises

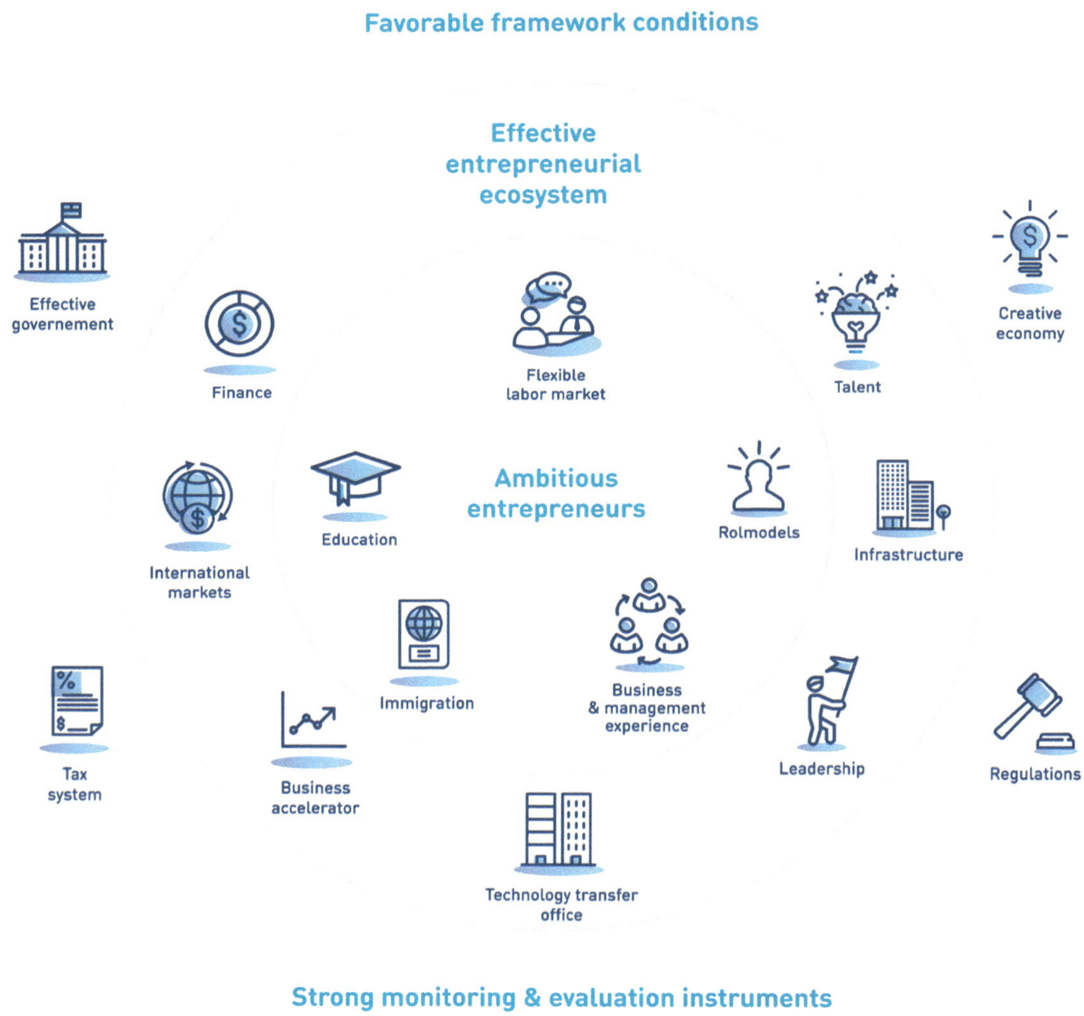

Source: UNECE, adapted from (Ratinckx & Raspoet, 2018).

1.3 Innovative high-growth enterprises in the EESC sub-region – the state of play

Data on high-growth enterprises, especially over time in the six EESC countries, is very limited[10]. None of the countries have official statistics on high-growth firms related to:

- the prevalence of high-growth enterprises in the economy;
- employment in high-growth enterprises and its share in total employment;
- sets of panel data tracking firm growth over time.

Data on high-growth enterprises for the EU suggest that the employment share of high-growth enterprises measured in employment (number of employees working at high-growth enterprises divided by the total number of employees working in active enterprises with at least 10 employees) is on average just over 15 per cent (2017) with a variation ranging from 7.65 per cent in Romania to close to 25 per cent in Ireland. While high-growth enterprises are normally present in all the sectors of a given economy, their share of employment is higher on average in the information and communication sector and other professional, scientific and technical activities (Eurostat)[11]. In a similar vein, the European Scale-Up Report[12] (analysing scale-ups[13] founded between 2007 and 2013) identified 80,000 scale-ups in eight European countries that are primarily involved in business products and services (30 per cent), consumer goods and services (26 per cent), construction (17 per cent), ICT (12 per cent), transportation (6 per cent) or biotech and healthcare (4 per cent). Hence, **the sectoral distribution of high-growth firms is not confined to technology-intensive sectors but is spread throughout a given economy**.

In EESC economies the share of high-growth enterprises and their sectoral distribution is likely to be influenced by factors such as the existing economic structure, societal trends, priorities and so forth in each country. In the absence of reliable data for the EESC sub-region, we gathered evidence from the interviewees, who pointed to the emergence of a specific "tech niche" (linked to the national start-up ecosystems), the potential for existing enterprises in certain product or service markets to scale-up internationally as well as the scope for building on national strengths or through spin-offs from large public or foreign owned firms. Table 1.1 provides an overview of the identified areas in which the most potential exists for IHGEs in each EESC country. **A common theme across all six countries is the growth in their digital sectors including business software services, online financial services, e-commerce and the like**. This focus is partly due to the existing 'specialisations' in terms of the knowledge base and talent in the six countries but also reflects the easier scalability of digital solutions. Nevertheless, the review of IHGE potential underlines the scope for development in manufacturing, engineering, agricultural, energy sectors often by integrating digital or other advanced technologies into existing business practices, e.g. Fintech[14] or Medtech[15].

Table 1.1 Potential high-growth ecosystems in the EESC sub-region

Country	Main business ecosystems with high growth potential	Examples of innovative high-growth enterprises
Armenia	Main segments of activity for tech companies are in **software applications and digital services** (e-commerce, management systems, financial, etc.) (EU SMEDA, 2019). **Biotech solutions, Cleantech and seismic engineering** are examples of vertical applications with high potential for Armenia's software and hardware developers (World Bank, 2020). **Precision engineering** is an important sector for the Armenian economy and has good development and export potential (EU SMEDA, 2017).	Although it was launched in 2012 in San Francisco, **PicsArt**[a] has most of its operations and employees in Armenia. PicsArt provides an all-in-one photo and video editing app for making social content. With more than 150 million monthly active creators, the PicsArt community creates, remixes and shares nearly 1 billion images every month and is available in over 30 languages. PicsArt's annual revenues are about $15m. **SoloLearn**[b] is a US-Armenian company founded in 2014. It is the largest mobile social platform for coders around the globe to consume, create, and share programming content. **Krisp**[c] is a noise-cancelling app that mutes background noise during calls over Skype, Slack or other VoIP services. This Armenian-American start-up has raised US$5 million[d], the company reportedly went from 0 to 600 paying enterprises and from US$0 to US$4 million annual revenue in a single year as demand soared in part due to the boom in home-office work resulting from the COVID-19 crisis.
Azerbaijan	The Innovation Agency has identified 200 start-up firms and characterized them from early stage to mature. They are drawn from a variety of sectors, however, **digital solutions tend to dominate.** Among the priority areas for further development, as defined by the Government and the Innovation Agency, are **renewable energy, Fintech and Biotech** with application to Medtech and Agritech (e.g. bioplastics).	Role model examples include several foreign based Azerbaijanis such as the founder of **Evernote** and the recent acquisition by Twitter of an ad-management platform developed by an Azerbaijani software engineer. **Keepface**[e] is an automated platform for brands to reach the most relevant influencers, communicate with them and manage campaigns using real-time analytics. **Wasco Labs** combines unique ultrasonic Smart Sensors that monitor waste collection in real-time using the Internet of Things (IoT) or mobile data with sophisticated software (Smart Analytics, Smart Route Planner and Smart Management system) providing cities and businesses with data-driven decision making and optimization of waste collection routes, frequencies and vehicle loads[f] **B.EST Solutions**[g] founded in 2009, is a fast-growing IT-services company and solutions provider active in the ICT field in the Republics of Estonia and Azerbaijan. It provides national digital identity and legally binding e-signatures based on Mobile-ID technology branded "Asan Imza" operated from the Republic of Azerbaijan. The company has recently supported the launch of the Digital Trade Hub[h] and of the m-residency initiative in Azerbaijan modelled on the Estonian e-residency programme.
Belarus	The focus in Belarus has been on the **IT field** with over 100,000 people employed nationally in the sector, although the sector faces challenges to remain competitive. The potential for growth in traditionally strong sectors such as advanced instruments/equipment (e.g. Adani), **mechanical engineering** (agricultural and transport related production) or pharmaceuticals also exist. Other niche areas with potential high-growth include **retail, textiles and the food sector** (OECD, 2020).	**Adani Systems** - a science-based industrial enterprise created in the 1990s and focused on R&D and manufacturing of high-tech, science-based equipment for medical radiology, X-ray security screening, non-destructive testing, radiation control and ESR spectrometry. **Mediacube** is an international company and an official partner of both YouTube and TikTok. It is among the top 25 video content copyright holders in the world. Mediacube is engaged in the monetization of video/music content. **Amasty**[i] is a leading e-commerce stores. They offer more than 250 extensions and solutions to suit any eCommerce business. Created in 2009, Amasty now partners with 280+ companies worldwide. The company's certified developers customize and implement projects of varying complexity. **Uniflex** is a full cycle flexo-graphic printing house, the leader in the Belarusian flexo-printing market and one of the largest printing companies in the Commonwealth of Independent States.

Table 1.1 Potential high-growth ecosystems in the EESC sub-region (Concluded)

Country	Main business ecosystems with high growth potential	Examples of innovative high-growth enterprises
Georgia	The country has an ICT cluster[j] combining 11 companies developing a technology platform. **The Fintech field** is viewed as a potential source of IHGEs along with the application of skills in mathematics and **AI**. **Agrifood tech** holds further potential (e.g. health and nutrition products) building on the existing strong food sector. Other examples include the application of digital solutions to develop travel tech applications (e.g. for adventure tourism).	**Phubber**[k] is a digital marketplace that connects people who want to buy and sell clothes and accessories. The platform hosts Georgian designers' collections, vintage pieces, mass-market brands, outlets, authentic brands and second hand for clothes and footwear. The company has attracted more than GEL 1 million in starting capital through a Bank of Georgia investment, obtained as part of the 500 Start-up accelerator programme. Phubber has a strong position in the Georgian market but has the objective to scale-up to be an international company and penetrate the markets of the other countries in the region and Eastern Europe to attract approximately 25 million registered users. **SensorGe**[l] has developed a concept of sensor or touch-free buttons. The innovation was awarded a small grant via GITA. The company has already commenced production, modifying and developing various touch-free buttons for elevators which, topically, minimises virus infections risks.
Moldova	Key sectors with growth potential include: • **Electronics and IT** (software) – start-ups in e-commerce, the IoT and AI. • Foodtech • **Textiles and design**	**Endeva**[m] is a publicly-listed software development company, founded in 2000 in London and Moldova. **Salt-Edge Inc.** is an industry-leading financial technology company with offices in Toronto, London and Chisinau. **Simpals**[n] is a group of Moldovan companies which provides online services and one of the largest animation studios in the sub-region. Simpals is the leader in the online advertising market in Moldova and owns the largest portals, including the most visited Moldovan site 999.md. Founded in 2002, Simpals Studio made its debut in Moldovan market by producing commercials and music videos for several local bands.
Ukraine	Strong **ICT/software cluster** based on a talent pool fostered by the education sector but largely dominated by IT services and outsourcing. Other sectors with potential growth through technology upgrading include **natural resource-based sectors, machinery and equipment** (World Bank, 2019) and also **energy and agri-food.**	**Grammarly** (a digital writing assistant, has raised a total investment of US$200 million) and **GitLab** (a DevOps platform and application has raised US$436 million) are both considered as Ukranian unicorns. **Preply** is an online educational platform that pairs students with private tutors remotely via online chat. It features a ranking algorithm that uses machine learning for the classification and recommendation of tutors. **GreenFuel** produces, installs and maintains electric charging stations in Ukraine and other European countries. The company was founded in 2014, raised US$100,000 and successfully operates a network of electric vehicle charging stations along with developing software for controlling the charging process[o].

Source: Author's analysis for UNECE.
[a] https://picsart.com
[b] https://www.sololearn.com/
[c] https://krisp.ai/
[d] See: https://techcrunch.com/2020/08/05/krisp-snags-5m-a-round-as-demand-grows-for-its-voice-isolating-algorithm/
[e] https://keepface.com
[f] https://wascolabs.com/about
[g] https://bestsolutions.az/
[h] https://azertag.az/en/xeber/Digital_Trade_Hub_of_Azerbaijan_and_Asan_Imza_presented_at_United_Nations_2020_SPECA_ECONOMIC_FORUM-1648959
[i] https://amasty.com/
[j] https://ictcluster.ge
[k] https://phubber.ge/
[l] https://sensorge.com/
[m] www.endeva.com
[n] https://simpals.com/en/ & https://simpals.studio/
[o] https://greenfuel.in.ua/

Notes

1 See for instance, the data compiled by the Harvard Growth Lab on trade flows in products and services based on their 'complexity': https://atlas.cid.harvard.edu/

2 In line with the Global Entrepreneurship Monitor distinction of whether an entrepreneur starts a business to take advantage of a business opportunity or because they have no other options to secure work or an income.

3 For example, the impact of IHGEs on the US economy was analysed in a study covering the period 1998-2008. The study showed that this group of firms was responsible for the generation of almost 100 per cent of all net jobs created in the economy over the indicated period. The subset of high-impact enterprises is also characterized by high growth rates and an ability to generate more revenue on average with the same input in terms of human capital (Tracey, 2011).

4 As defined by the Eurostat-OECD, gazelles are the subset of high-growth enterprises that are up to 5 years old with average annualised growth greater than 20% per annum, over a three-year period.

5 Disruptive Innovations are not necessarily breakthrough technologies; rather they are innovations that make products and services more accessible and affordable, thereby making them available to a larger population. See for instance: https://hbr.org/2015/12/what-is-disruptive-innovation

6 Using the DynEMP database on employment dynamics and the economic effects of start-up firms.

7 In some countries, such as France, more stringent labour market regulations apply to companies with 50 or more employees, leading many firms to artificially cap their expansion, i.e. not going over 49 employees.

8 The study analysed the situation in eight countries, i.e. Germany, France, the United Kingdom, Poland, Switzerland, the USA, South Korea and Japan.

9 Skills that are cross-cutting across jobs and sector and relate to personal competence (confidence, discipline, self-management) and social competences (teamwork, communication, emotional intelligence).

10 See for instance the OECD Compendiums of Enterprise Statistics for Armenia and Ukraine

11 See: https://ec.europa.eu/eurostat/web/products-datasets/product?code=bd_9pm_r2

12 See: https://www.scale-ups.eu/the-scale-up-landscape/2020/european-scale-up-report-2019

13 For this report, scale-ups were defined as companies that had raised at least US$1 million in funding since their foundation and an average annualized growth rate of at least 20 per cent per annum over a three-year period.

14 Innovative applications of digital technology for financial services, or Fintech, are used to alter the interface between financial consumers and service providers and help to improve communication with consumers and increase their engagement.

15 Medical technology, or «Medtech», encompasses a wide range of healthcare products and is used to treat diseases and medical conditions affecting humans.

Part II

POLICIES TO PROMOTE IHGES

2.1 The rationale for policy intervention:

Box 2.1 Innovative high-growth enterprises

IHGEs are inherently different from SMEs, making many standard support measures broadly aimed at SMEs relatively ineffective. A first step is to integrate IHGE-related concerns into the overall effort to improve the business climate as well as the improving access to soft (e.g. training for skills) and hard (e.g. technology and innovation centres) infrastructure. This needs to be done in concert with introducing and scaling up measures and mechanisms for targeted support of businesses carefully tailored towards mitigating constraints and reducing inordinate risks that hold back innovation with high potential spill-over effects. Such initiatives should consider:

- ***Who to support?*** *Analysis of a set of "trigger points" may help identify potential IHGEs before they start growing and help with the design successful policies.*
- ***What policy?*** *Addressing barriers to growth at each step of firms' development is a crucial element.*
- ***How to support?*** *Government should be playing a "coordinator" role, enhancing links between the potential IHGEs and resources critical for their growth in terms of scale-up expertise, talented employees and growth capital.*

Policies to catalyse and support business growth have been around for decades, especially in developed countries. A plethora of studies have looked at the rationale for policies, types of policy support and, to a lesser extent, their effectiveness. Over the past few decades, attention has shifted away **from supporting individual companies to creating an enabling environment or 'innovation ecosystem'** (Grover Goswami & Olafsen, 2019) **in which entrepreneurs starting a potential high-growth firm or existing firms with growth or scaling potential can prosper.** Although most elements of such an enabling environment are beneficial for IHGEs, as they are for the private sector overall, the "*main difference between targeted support programmes for potential IHGEs and wider business support lies in selectivity*" ((OECD, 2020).

The questions to keep in mind when designing IHGE policies are summarized below.

Figure 2.1 • Why, who, what, how of IHGE policy

Why ?
Optimising the economy wide transformative effects of innovative firms with growth potential.

Who ?
Selectivity by applying objective criteria for targeting innovative firms with growth potential.

What ?
The mix of support measures tailored to the growth stages and specific needs of targeted firms.

How ?
The delivery of the policy intervention by one or more organisations.

Source: UNECE

2.1.1 Why (should Government support IHGEs)?

As discussed in Part 1, a policy based on identifying upfront companies that have growth potential and that seeks to intervene in a timely manner to ensure their growth occurs is a complex and risky (as a venture capitalist (VC) would confirm) undertaking that requires strong institutional capacities within the organizations that will be providing support. Indeed, *"high-growth potential is only one side of the coin, the other is a clear focus on social return of the investment. This means that the initiative, if successful, is likely to have some kind of positive effect on broader parts of the economy. This could involve anything from demonstrating the viability of a technology, encouraging other SMEs to adopt it, to creating a completely new sector in the economy"* ((OECD, 2018).

Adopting an "economic transformation" perspective to the why question also helps broaden the classic 'market failure' argument for public intervention. Three main types of market failure are commonly used to justify state intervention.

- **Externalities.** The main reason for the existence of negative externalities is the difficulty to exclusively own the outcome of one's (knowledge) investment, i.e. innovation is easily copied once proven commercially viable.
- **Uncertainty.** It is a natural part of any innovation process and results in a market failure because it produces information asymmetries.
- **Indivisibility.** Economies of scale are needed to justify investment. However, questions as to the required scale of production for breaking even on an innovation arise (e.g. the firm having the appropriate financial capacity to scale).

The outcome is that the rational decisions of individual entrepreneurs or businesses lead to situations that are unfavourable (lower investment in innovation) from a societal point of view. **Innovative firms with high-growth potential are particularly vulnerable to market failures and this may discourage entrepreneurs from engaging in an innovative venture given the uncertainty about the chances of a profitable outcome.** However, beyond the standard market failures, **system failures** (coordination (institutional), capability, network and infrastructural failures) and **transformational failures** (that impede the transformation of systems of production and consumption, e.g. energy systems) can further constrain both innovation and business growth (Arnold, 2014). Table 2.1 summarises potential failures and their relevance for the EESC sub-region. In particular, the capacity to absorb new knowledge is crucial to any firm's success and participation in a network of relationships with other organizations increases the chance that they will find or develop capacities to achieve growth. Failures due to the lack of an effective institutional (regulatory) environment or the required 'infrastructure', notably in the areas of education, training and investment in basic science that enable firms to develop, can also impede the potential for IHGEs in a country. Moreover, (Mazzucato, 2015) has stressed that the **emphasis should not be just on fixing market failures or minimizing government failures but "on maximising the transformative impact of policy that can shape and create markets".**

In this context, the relevant question for a policymaker is not 'which are the high-growth firms in my economy', but rather 'which are the firms with high-growth potential that do not grow because of the existence of market or system failures that policy could correct'. **The firms to be targeted are not those that would grow in any case but those for which policy intervention would make a difference**.

Table 2.1 Responding to market and system failures to release the IHGE potential

Type of failure	Description	Relevance to the EESC sub-region and policy responses
Externalities	It is too difficult to appropriate enough of the results of innovation to make private investment worthwhile. Innovation is easy for competitors to copy and there are limited opportunities to protect new ideas.	In terms of access to finance for R&D and innovation, the situation in most EESC countries is sub-optimal, and while seed funding is available, grant or equity finance for subsequent stages of product or service development are limited.
Barriers to competition	Market power (for example, through the first supplier building an insurmountable advantage) may lead to consumer lock-in. High cost of market entry/exit due to, for example, large incumbent firms (including state owned enterprises). Uncertainty about or lack of a market for products/services. Investment does not occur because there is no established market with predictable prices for the products/services in question.	IHGEs in emerging technology fields or those based on new business models that challenge incumbents (e.g. energy firms) will often struggle to break into even national markets, never mind go global. The role of the public sector as a source of demand (innovative public procurement) for new innovative solutions can help create new markets.
Information (knowledge) asymmetries	High levels of specialized technical, financial and/or market knowledge mean that not all economic actors involved in a given process have a sound basis for making informed decisions. Actors optimize locally, based on what they currently know rather than all the available information.	Access to specialized know-how is not always readily available in all countries. Interviewees underlined the need for improved knowledge of international markets and tech trends. Publicly supported access to market and technology advice can be critical for decision making at the key stages of growth.
Institutional failures	Institutions (both in the sense of 'organizations' and 'rules and conventions') can operate in ways that impede innovation. Rules and regulations may not be conducive to innovation and business development. Government policy may have the same effect.	Interviewees stressed that the current institutional framework in the EESC sub-region did not favour the creation and growth of IHGEs. Further improvements to regulatory frameworks could help boost the potential for sustained growth.
Capability failures	These failures result from the difference between the capabilities of real firms and those of an idealized economic model, so that firms lack the needed skills, resources, ability to learn, absorptive and analytic capacity to exploit innovation opportunities.	Potential IHGEs in the EESC sub-region are unlikely to have 'in-house' all the capabilities required to help them grow. Mentoring and strategic advice can be made available to IHGEs – this can be done through structures such as accelerators, etc.
Network failures	IHGEs may be in networks that are fragmented or within which communication and cooperation may be poor. Networks may be locked into technological regimes and markets or products that make it difficult to transition to new technologies or business models.	The EESC countries are at the geographical crossroads of various trading blocs – access to international business and innovation networks is not always easy. Governments can support improved access for IHGEs to relevant initiatives, establish networks of diaspora experts, etc.
Infrastructural failures	Insufficient investment by the state in human capital and in knowledge infrastructures critical to innovation performance, for example, regarding education and skills, basic research, etc. This failure varies by business sector (e.g. emerging sectors may face more of a challenge) and depends on past investments in each country.	Access to (both technical and soft) skills was underlined by interviewees as an issue; the weakness of the R&D system in the EESC sub-region was pinpointed as a significant barrier for tech-based IHGEs. Targeted investments (public-private) in upgrading skills as well as research and innovation (demonstration, testing, fab labs, etc.) can help address these failures.

Source: UNECE, based on (Arnold, 2014).

2.1.2 Who (which firms)?

Identifying IHGEs

IHGE policy is not about 'picking winners' but about going a step beyond standard entrepreneurship and SME development policies. The aim is to target a group of firms that have one or more characteristics that suggest they may grow rapidly and contribute to the economic dynamism and transformation of the given regional and national economy. The required public intervention required is thus more akin to the logic of a venture capitalist who invests in a portfolio knowing that not all the businesses will grow and generate high returns. Hence, a "key issue in high-growth policy is therefore how to identify firms with the potential for high growth given that the potential for high growth is neither visible nor measurable, and that high growth itself exhibits little persistence" (OECD, 2013).

A clear understanding of what defines IHGEs is important for the purpose of tracking the success of policies via robust statistical data. However, first and foremost, **understanding how to identify a potential IHGE serves as the foundation to design appropriate policies to support these entrepreneurs and thereby help drive national structural transformation and long-term sustainable development**. The characteristics to be used when identifying potential IHGEs may be derived from a range of trigger points (OECD, 2018) and employed to design successful IHGEs support programmes (Table 2.2).

Developing a targeted approach for support

In line with the information presented above, enterprise and innovation agencies in OECD countries tend to adopt a **segmentation strategy** to tailor support packages to the needs of companies based on the individual company's characteristics. **Segmentation implies that an agency looks at a portfolio of companies it wishes to influence and breaks them down according to a set of characteristics.** This process then leads to differentiated offers per target segment, each offer being tailored to maximize the impact and be optimally suited to each set of clients. Segmentation also enables an agency to tailor its support to specific targeted needs within a segment which, hopefully in turn, further increases the efficiency of the support provided.

Targeting does not mean leaving out certain sectors as IHGEs can be anywhere

Targeting firms according to defined "growth potential" characteristics does not imply a focus, or at least not an over-emphasis, on specific sectors or on start-up firms. All ICT or biotech start-ups or firms are no more likely to achieve high growth than all food manufacturers or equipment suppliers. As has been previously mentioned, IHGEs are present across all sectors and while they are usually 'young' this is different from being a start-up. Indeed, there are many examples of firms growing rapidly at different 'ages' linked to the trigger points mentioned above. For example, a family-owned business may experience high-growth when a son or daughter takes over from the parent who founded the company. Hence, the question of which firms are likely to grow is independent of their age and sector. Rather the key deciding factor is the innovative nature of the products and services offered or being developed. **Policy should seek to assist both start-ups and**

Table 2.2 Examples of trigger points to identify potential IHGEs

Kinds of triggers	Examples	Explanation
Organizational changes	Changes in ownership, buy-outs, new investors.	Top management or ownership changes normally go along with substantial changes to the way business is conducted, this may have high-growth potential and need targeted support to take off.
Business model changes	New markets, production methods, the introduction of concerted customer relationship management; new channels, such as e-commerce; internationalization, etc.	High growth comes from a clear commitment to trying new things. Often, these are new products – but innovation can also come from new channels, new markets, or closer interaction with existent customers.
Investments	Investment in new technology; introduction of enterprise resource planning (ERP) or other core business process software.	Substantial new investments can be a clear signal of growth ambitions.
Product changes	Introduction of products (services) new to the market; substantial upgrading of existing products (services).	IHGEs should be investing in product development (and on-going tailoring of their products to evolving customer needs) as well as in in-house innovation or partnerships with external R&D or technology suppliers.
Changes in domestic and/ or international markets	Uptake of certain global trends in market demand, business processes, etc. (e.g. increased use of platforms) that shape demand and offer domestic opportunities, creating new market niches with high potential for growth.	The high growth of innovative ventures can happen in response to global market trends and the development of such in domestic economies (uptake of platforms, Uber for example, has been challenged by an Estonian competitor Bolt; rising demand from the German automotive industry contributed to the high growth of the automotive sector in Moldova).
Attitudes	A clear desire and ambition for double-digit growth, innovation and willingness to try out new ideas. This is partly a subjective criterion but can be validated via assessments by qualified business advisors (e.g. from high-growth support initiatives).	IHGEs need entrepreneurs with clear, ambitious vision and a desire to try out new activities to lead them.

Source: UNECE, based on (OECD, 2018).

existing firms to scale-up and exploit their potential. At the same time, there is a good reason to add the expected growth potential of certain sectors, products or services as a characteristic for identifying potential IHGEs due to forecast trends in regional or global markets. The combination of targeted support for potential IHGEs and priority sectors or an emerging niche that offers the most potential for economic transformation can ensure a cost-effective policy intervention (e.g. in the Scottish case, support for potential high-growth firms is aligned with seven national priority programmes in areas such as zero emission, hydrogen economy or future medicines)[1].

Figure 2.2 · Example of segmentation of an enterprise agency's client base

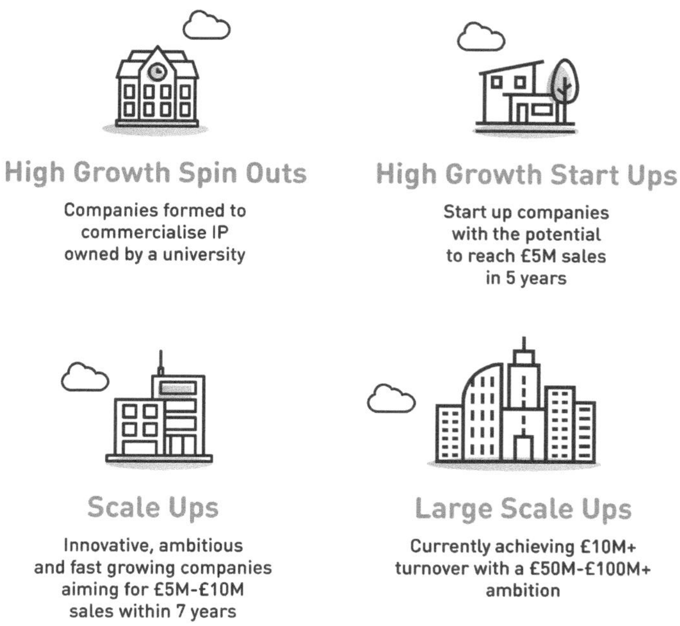

Source: UNECE, adapted from Scottish Enterprise (https://www.scottish-enterprise.com/support-for-businesses/business-development-and-advice/scale-your-business)

2.1.3 What (sort of support is required)?

Policy support for IHGEs should be viewed as part of a larger effort of related measures taken to support and encourage firms to innovate, grow, export, etc. In this regard though, a useful distinction can be made between four 'levels' of policy intervention (Figure 2.3).

SMEs, entrepreneurship, and effective IHGE support measures differ substantially

Measures designed to support IHGEs fall into the fourth category cited above, namely targeted measures. Very often, however, governments overlook IHGEs when designing SME or entrepreneurship policies with the expectation that the same policy tools used to support SMEs or start-ups are suitable for IHGEs. As the body of literature demonstrates, **IHGEs are different from standard SMEs in many ways and need targeted support to provide for their needs and enable growth and, as such, most SME policies fall short of providing that kind of support** (Table 2.3).

Market validation as a central indicator for ensuring the impact of support measures

In reality, there is often a lack of clarity about policies that target (innovative) start-ups and policies that target the scaling up of firms with high-growth ambitions and a business model that has been 'market validated'. Most start-ups will either not manage to validate the scalable nature of the business model or not achieve the growth they initially expected (Calvino, 2016). **The market validation of the business model (or innovative product**

Figure 2.3 • Levels of policy support to firms

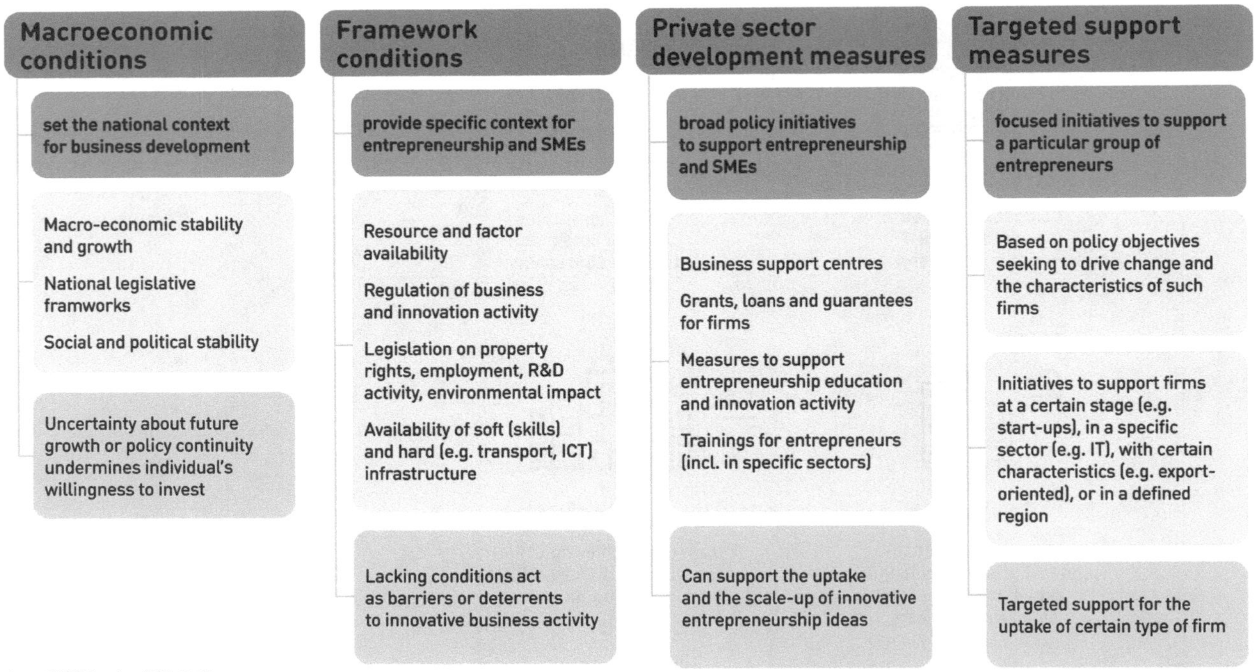

Source: UNECE, based on (OECD, 2013).

or service) is a central criterion that helps both private investors and government-backed services target potential IHGEs. This handbook addresses policy-related issues for enterprises that have ambitions to scale and have a scalable business model, irrespective of whether such businesses are start-ups or established firms.

Growth is facilitated by a strong ecosystem for scaling up

As it is difficult to identify, *ex-ante*, the firms that will scale and achieve high growth, policy interventions may focus on **addressing barriers to growth at different stages in the development of IHGEs**. It is important to emphasize that a conducive business ecosystem for scaling up should readily support the transition from one growth stage to the next and to do so, the ecosystem needs to facilitate the inevitable changes in company management and on the investor side (IRIS Group, 2019). Needless to say, these stages are illustrative and real life does not follow a linear trajectory. For instance, the need to think about broadening management (from (an) initial founder(s) and developing organisational structures should begin as soon as required and not only when a firm enters the expansion phase. Similarly, talent shows up at unlikely times and the firm should seek to capture it when it can. Network building can start immediately or come later (e.g. due to the need to either work through an open innovation process or protect business secret or IP during development) but should be a constant focus of attention.

At each stage, the type of support will evolve and change in line with the evolving needs of the IHGE. As growth may be rapid, this requires a flexible and tailored approach that often is best coordinated by an 'account (or client) manager' in the agency mandated to support, applying a **portfolio approach** (support instruments available from different sources and enjoying varying levels of subsidy are drawn together to cover different strategic priorities, different stages of the IHGE development) (OECD, 2018).

Table 2.3 Stylized differences among typical SME, entrepreneurship and IHGE support measures

Type	SME policies	Entrepreneurship	IHGE policies
Target of measure	Existing SMEs, including micro-enterprises and sole traders	Potential entrepreneurs and start-ups	SMEs with the potential and ambition to grow fast
Rationale	Sustain jobs, reduce poverty, support underdeveloped regions and the employment of women, young people or disadvantaged groups	Focus on unleashing entrepreneurial capacity, in a gender balanced way, facilitating start-ups that help maintain a vibrant SME base	Contributing to structural transformation by shifting the economy towards higher productivity activities and growth in the share of skilled jobs
Objective	Create a level playing-field and ensure SME survival or mitigate the social consequences of structural change	More start-ups in the economy	More high-growth firms in the economy
Nature of support	Financial incentives; regulatory simplification	Training, match-making, and facilities for incubation	Advisory and peer support to management teams; policy advocacy to remove constraints to growth
Eligibility	All or most SMEs; sometimes limited to women or underrepresented groups	All entrepreneurs; sometimes limited to women or the ICT sector	Limited eligibility, decided on a case-by-case basis with criteria strongly correlated with subsequent high growth
Examples: Access to finance	Credit guarantees; direct soft loans	Subsidies for seed funding	Matching IHGEs with sources of finance; enabling environment and limited direct investment into risk finance
Examples: Building capacities	Generic training on business planning, accounting, HR management, and process automation	Entrepreneurship training; mentoring mechanisms	Targeted training and interventions depending on the business life cycle and subject to strict performance requirements
Examples: Business climate	Comprehensive view of business climate reform, e.g. the issues monitored in the World Bank Doing Business report	Less of an emphasis; focus on business start-up regulations	Very targeted to specific constraints that, as a result of analysis and consultation, appear to hold back potential high-growth ventures
Limitations and risks	Deadweight losses and displacement effects; may slow down efficient resource reallocation by keeping less productive enterprises running	Most start-ups fail or stagnate; e.g. venture capitalists calculate that 90 per cent of investments will not perform	Predicting high growth is difficult. Effective targeted support can be costly, and the effects hard to measure. Risk of creating entrenched privileges (but can be offset by monitoring if firms reach growth targets.
Institutions	Standard SME agencies, with divisions for business climate reform, BDS and access to finance	Separate agencies, mostly with a specific purpose such as incubation	Autonomous agencies employing a key account logic and with officials getting to know entrepreneurs as well as their activities while accompanying them throughout a business' life cycle.
Processes	Standard processes, with long-term and yearly work plans and indicators such as the number of SMEs supported	Advisory and mentoring support, generally for a short period (several months to a year) aimed at supporting the entrepreneur to launch a start-up	Focus on key account logic. The need for continuous internal and external monitoring and evaluation with performance criteria that, if not reached, lead to the discontinuation of support

Source: UNECE, based on (OECD, 2018).

Figure 2.4 • Start-ups and scale-ups — the importance of validating the business model

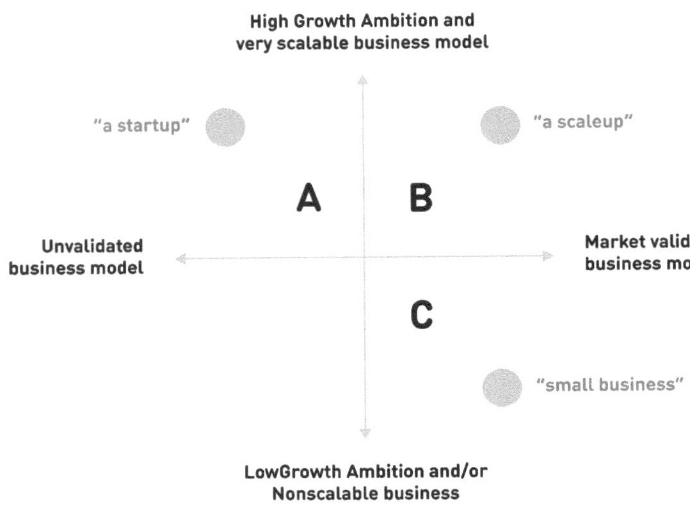

Source: UNECE, adapted from (Zhao, 2019).

Figure 2.5 • Stages of growth

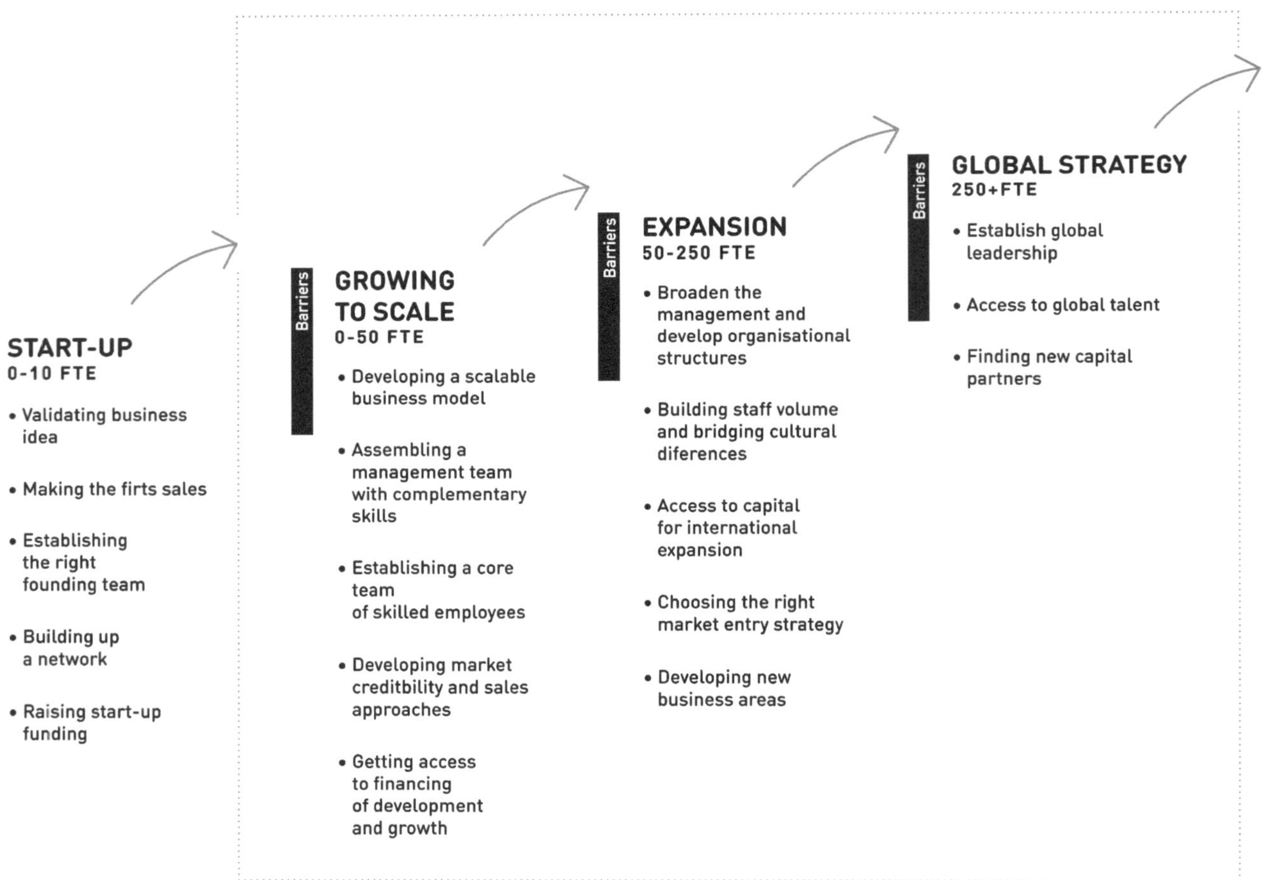

Source: UNECE, adapted from (IRIS Group, 2019).
Note: FTE = full time equivalent employees.

2.1.4 How (channels can deliver the support)?

Compared to established firms focused on national or a limited number of export markets, **IHGEs require a differentiated and tailored portfolio of investment advice and mentoring**. From a Government budget perspective, this need not imply large financial outlays as the key support for IHGEs is often of an advisory, peer-to-peer or mentoring nature. When finance is required, the focus should be on leveraging private investment through creating the right framework for investors to step-in and help IHGEs grow.

Ensuring IHGEs are able to access resources critical for their growth

Recent reviews of high-growth enterprise policy concur that the **primary focus needs to be on building stronger 'ecosystems' by enhancing the links between potential IHGEs and the critical resources they need to scale successfully – primarily access to scale-up expertise, talented employees and growth capital** (IRIS Group, 2019). Similarly, (Grover Goswami & Olafsen, 2019) recommend that governments focus on the "ABCs" of growth entrepreneurship, namely improving Allocative efficiency (firms need to access capital, skilled people, etc.), encouraging Business-to-business (B2B) connectivity and spill-overs, and strengthening firms' Capabilities.

Figure 2.6 • Three entry points for effective IHGE support policies

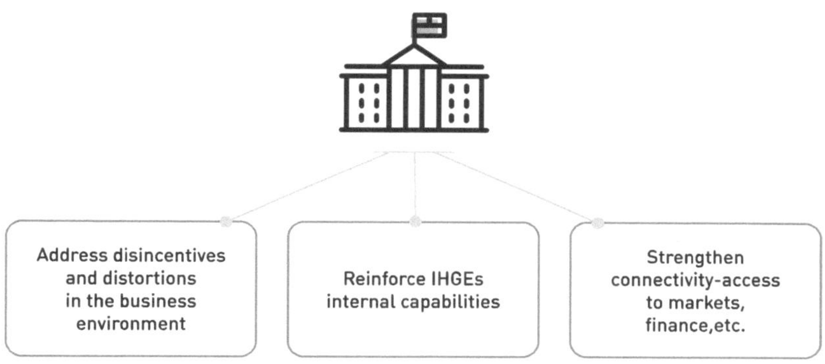

Source: UNECE

Delivering effective public support to IHGEs

This section examines in more detail the 'how' question by exploring different policy interventions that can be mobilized to support IHGEs. However, for the effective use of public funds it is critical to ensure that IHGE policy is designed and implemented within a **robust institutional environment, adapted to the national context** and **respects the principles of additionality** (support should leverage rather than replace or crowd out private investment) **as well as neutrality** (firms supported are selected based on their potential for growth and in line with clear and transparent criteria).

In most countries, the organizations responsible for coordinating the delivery of public support to IHGEs will be either departments (units) of national (and/or in larger countries, regional) enterprise and innovation agencies; state-owned financial intermediaries (such as investment banks or export credit agencies) as well as a range of accredited organizations that may receive some public funding to provide mentoring and advisory services to IHGEs.

Beyond the role of the public agencies, the organizations that should be available to support IHGEs range from **equity investors, business accelerators, executive education and tailored training via business schools through to scale-up initiatives, growth mentoring programmes and peer networks** (including international networks) etc. In all the countries highlighted in the table above, the government agency plays a role of a coordinator of support (and a provider of funding) rather than being the sole provider of expertise. Examples of initiatives are provided in the subsequent sections to help illustrate the types of services and support as well as how they can be best organized and delivered to IHGEs.

Table 2.4 Examples of delivery agencies for IHGE type initiatives in selected countries

Country	Agency	Dedicated programme or department
Estonia	**Enterprise Estonia (EAS)**[a] is a national foundation that aims to develop Estonia's economy through three principal areas of activity: Developing Estonian enterprises and boosting export capacity; increasing tourism revenue; bringing high value-added foreign investments to Estonia.	Enterprise Development Programme – supports ambitious enterprises with the readiness to invest and desire to grow, develop and launch new products and services. It provides both funding and advisory services.
Finland	**Business Finland**[b] provides support for enterprises for R&D work and helps them to grow and assists their efforts to expand internationally. It provides expert services in target countries and information about international markets. **Finnvera**[c] - a specialized state-owned financing company and the official export credit agency.	Growth Engines - supports growth of platform companies and the related ecosystem Advisory services for international growth Growth Loan – a debt-based mezzanine financing product
Scotland	**Scottish Enterprise**[d] is Scotland's national economic development agency. It delivers a range of funding and advisory services to businesses.	Support for scale-ups – offering tailored packages of advisory and skill development services. Grant and loan funding from Scottish Enterprise or other agencies can be mobilized.
Singapore	**Enterprise Singapore**[e] is a government agency championing enterprise development. They work with committed companies to build capabilities, innovate and internationalize. They also support the growth of Singapore as a hub for global trading and start-ups.	Scale-up SG – peer learning and collaboration plus advice from a network public and private sector partners.

Source: Author's analysis for UNECE.
[a] https://www.eas.ee/eas/?lang=en
[b] https://www.businessfinland.fi/en
[c] https://www.finnvera.fi/eng
[d] https://www.scottish-enterprise.com/
[e] https://www.scottish-enterprise.com/

2.2 A policy toolkit to foster IHGEs

Box 2.2 **A policy toolkit for innovative high growth enterprises**

The policy mix should aim to address a range of framework conditions and provide a set of resources that support the emergence and growth of innovative enterprises and help drive transformational change across an economy. Five main types of policy intervention are:

- A business environment that enables and promotes experimentation and growth;
- A portfolio of services tailored to the specific needs of IHGEs;
- The availability of finance for each growth stage of a IHGE;
- Improving firms''absorptive' capacities by ensuring they can recruit and train people with the skills required to drive and manage rapid growth;
- Access to services and networks that support scaling up internationally.

This section examines the main types of intervention that constitute a policy toolkit available to public policy stakeholders. The policy options are illustrated by examples from advanced economies (Nordic countries, Ireland, Singapore, the UK, etc.) as well as countries that have followed an economic-transition pathway, notably the Baltic States which are further along in a process similar to that which the EESC countries are going through.

When developing a policy to foster the development of IHGEs, two broad sets of factors should be kept in mind (IRIS Group, 2019):

- ***External (business environment) factors:*** institutions and regulations, access to finance, (international) business networks, availability of innovation infrastructures.
- ***Internal (company-level) factors:*** notably the 'absorptive capacity' (in terms of availability of people with skills to engage in design, production, finance, management and marketing) to support innovation and technological upgrading.

Furthermore, **policies for IHGEs should be co-designed and monitored in partnership with relevant stakeholders through a process of consultation to prioritise interventions and to rapidly adapt them to changing circumstances and past results.** Governments should put in place the necessary capacity to **design, deliver and evaluate IHGE policy**, including a robust evidence base (data on IHGEs, etc.), transparent and inclusive processes for designing and implementing policy as well as the procedures for evaluating their impacts.

Broadly speaking, there are **five types of policy intervention** that help optimize the growth potential of IHGEs as illustrated in the figure below.

Figure 2.8 • Five types of support measures for IHGEs

Pro-growth business environment	• Regulatory framework for innovation and growth • Taxation - incentivizing R&D and innovation and investors • Demand side measures - government as a first mover.
Tailored services for IHGEs	• High-growth programmes - client management approach • Developing business ecosystems and peer-to-peer networks • Access to innovation services and infrastructure
Finance adapted to each growth stage	• Grant and loan instruments • Crowdfunding, business angel investors & accelerators • Venture capital: co-investment and fund of funds models.
Reinforcing firms' internal capabilities to grow	• Leadership skills • Availability of employees with technical and creative skills • Talent attraction and retention
Internationalization & business networks that support scaling	• Advice on market trends and entry • International networks - structuring diaspora links.

Source: UNECE, based on (OECD, 2010) (European Commission, 2019) (IRIS Group, 2019) (Grover Goswami & Olafsen, 2019).

In more detail, the five main elements of the policy-kit are:

1. **Measures to foster a pro-growth business environment**. This first set of policy levers concern targeted improvements to the business environment that ***tackle productivity and growth limiting distortions***, in particular by addressing disincentives to growth present in legislation or regulations. These measures include:

    a. Encouraging entrepreneurial attitudes to stimulate more growth-oriented ambitions in new and existing businesses;

    b. Optimizing the legal and regulatory framework, including stimulating demand for innovative solutions;

    c. Ensuring the 'level playing field' conditions: rule of law, competition policy, labour markets, corporate law, tax system, etc.

2. **Delivering tailored services to IHGEs.** A targeted policy requires a dedicated ***set of "high-growth" mentoring and advisory services*** based on an accompanying set of instruments to support innovation (R&D, product development, piloting and testing). It also requires a certain quality of infrastructure and services available to enterprises conducting R&D and innovation.

3. **Policy measures enabling access to finance adapted to each growth stage:**
    a. Improving access to debt and equity finance for new and small firms to fund investment in R&D and the acquisition of non-tangible assets;
    b. Promoting the valuation of intellectual property and intangibles and their use as collateral for loans;
    c. Fostering an investor-friendly ecosystem and access to finance for IHGEs (including a role for accelerators, etc.);
    d. Improving the regulatory environment for investors (crowdfunding, angel investors, private equity funds) and finance tailored to scaling up IHGEs.
4. **Reinforcing the internal capabilities of a firm to grow.** This entails supporting the provision of training in growing enterprises, especially the management skills necessary to cope with the pressures on human, technical and financial resources created by business growth. Promoting a culture of change is a key element in the management of a growth process in a business of any age and size.
5. **Internationalization and business to business networks**. These measures include developing tailored advisory services for IHGEs such as trade facilitation, intellectual property rights advice (e.g. protecting trademarks in foreign markets), market analysis to support internationalization in regional and global markets.

The overall policy mix should seek to address a broad range of framework conditions that support the emergence and growth of innovative enterprises and help drive transformational change across an economy.

2.2.1 Measures to foster a pro-growth business environment

The environment for 'doing business' in the EESC countries is broadly positive (see the World Bank Doing Business[2] and (OECD, 2020) with some variations in overall performance and for specific indicators. However, there remain potential improvements that would significantly enhance the business environment and consequently, support the uptake of IHGEs. In all the EESC countries, the need to create the level playing-field conditions, accompanied by consistent enforcement of corruption and competition legislation is required to ensure business integrity, competitive neutrality and equal access to inputs and markets for all firms (OECD, 2020). (Grover Goswami & Olafsen, 2019) stress the importance of "allocative efficiency", which can be improved by tackling three broad policy "angles", namely improving the **ease of entry** for new and potentially more productive firms, **facilitating the exit** of less productive non-innovative firms and **improving access to resources** for existing firms looking to innovate through more flexible capital, labour and product market policies.

The interviewed stakeholders from the EESC sub-region underlined that the formalities for creating a company are not an issue for most businesses in the countries concerned (Georgia, Azerbaijan, Armenia and Moldova are all in the top 15 countries globally for starting a business in the World Bank's Doing Business rankings). However, for potential IHGEs seeking equity investors, the typical start-up route is to incorporate in the USA (Delaware) or in an EU country like Estonia (e.g. using e-residency) due to **the inadequate**

investor protection in EESC countries and the limited options for investors to exit (in the absence of functioning stock-markets for initial public offerings, etc.). Hence, it is critical to ensure that firms with high-growth potential, whether established nationally or incorporated abroad but operating locally, in sectors characterized by higher uncertainty and which potentially exhibit higher aggregate growth do not face additional regulatory or administrative barriers that reduce the allocative efficiency of scarce resources (e.g. ensuring that skilled labour or capital is being hired or invested into the potentially most productive firms in an economy).

It is important to underline that improvements to labour, investor or product market regulation does not equate to deregulation but better regulation. Four main types of policy measures can be applied to improve the legislative and regulatory environment for business growth and encourage innovation.

Figure 2.9 • Four key regulatory type measures

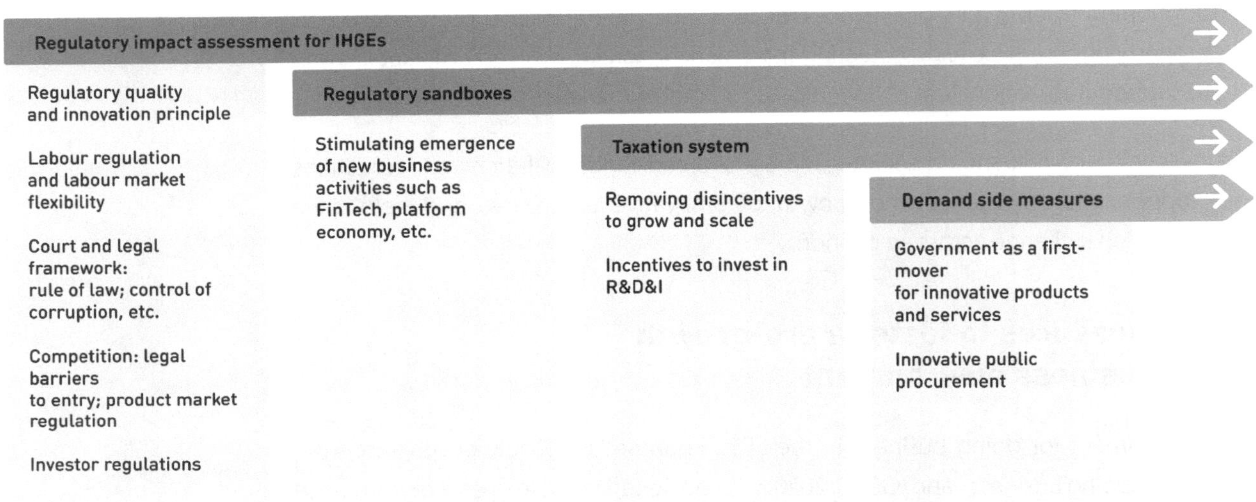

Source: UNECE

Regulatory impact assessment – taking account of the needs of IHGEs.

The first measure that can be taken is to review the current legislative and regulatory environment with respect to the specific difficulties it may pose for firms that are seeking to grow rapidly or for any disincentives the existing environment may create to scale-up or invest in IHGEs.

Regulatory impact assessment is a tool increasingly applied to avoid implementing legislation provisions that may adversely affect enterprises. **Regulation matters at all stages of the innovation process and it can be a powerful stimulus for innovation, however, regulation creating excessive administrative burdens and compliance costs for businesses may curtail the flow of resources devoted to innovation**. Regulation may hinder innovation if it is too prescriptive and inflexible as this limits the speed of technological progress or can increase uncertainty for investment (Simonelli & Renda, 2019). In the case of IHGEs, three regulatory aspects appear particularly important:

- The application of the 'innovation principle', which means that whenever a policy is developed, its impact on innovation is fully assessed;
- When the legislative process does not match the pace of innovation then the existing rules risk slowing down and disrupting innovation (the so-called pacing problem);
- Regulatory issues, including taxation, may provide a disincentive to scale-up or encourage growing firms to create subsidiaries rather than consolidating (e.g. more complex reporting obligations or higher taxation rates above a certain threshold).

Business growth, particularly if it is based on diversification or entry into new markets, will almost certainly lead to additional costs related to the process of learning and subsequent compliance with regulatory requirements that are new to the firm. However, IHGEs are more likely to be strategic in their approach to regulation and to recognize the competitive advantages that can be derived from having a good working knowledge of regulation. They are, therefore, pro-active learners in their approach to regulation (Peck, 2018).

Overall, less regulation does not necessarily mean more innovation and the ultimate impact of regulation on innovation needs to be carefully assessed on a case-by-case basis. Regulation, besides promoting innovation and its diffusion, can also provide direction to innovation, steering it towards specific societal needs. Good examples of this are environmental and data protection rules which have significantly affected the pace and direction of innovation in several domains.

The EU's Better Regulation Toolkit includes a Research and Innovation Tool[3] which can be used for analysing the interactions between new or revised legislation (including spending programmes) and innovation. It places emphasis on developing **future-proof regulation** and encourages the elimination of excessive compliance costs but does not embrace a de-regulatory stance (Simonelli & Renda, 2019). The box below provides an adapted version of the checklist tool that could be used by the EESC countries' national authorities.

Box 2.3 Regulation to foster innovation in the platform economy: the case of Estonia

In 2016, Estonia became the first European country to regulate and legalize ride and home sharing. The new rules put private hire drivers and taxis on common legal ground, with similar licensing and vetting requirements. The process for being qualified as taxi drivers were simplified and made less costly. Private hire drivers cannot pick up passengers who hail them in the street but they do not have to carry taxi signs or invest in a taxi meter (as consumers can verify such details via the app).

The results have been positive for the industry, the Government and consumers. The new rules have increased tax receipts, ride-hailing drivers are registered and reporting incomes for the first time and waiting times for rides in Tallinn have vanished. The Estonian ride-hailing platform Bolt has become a European unicorn: launched in 2013 by a 19-year-old high school student, it now operates in 150 cities across more than 35 countries, including 16 EU member states, and can lay claim to more than a million drivers and 30 million clients.

Source: UNECE, based on (Echikson, 2020)

Box 2.4 Adapted checklist for regulatory impact on research and innovation

Impact on R&D and innovation

- Does the measure affect the research, testing or demonstration phase?
- Does the measure potentially constrain innovative ideas, their adaptation and application in the country?
- Does it affect cooperation (e.g. data circulation of data, research results or skilled staff) between public/academic and corporate R&D?
- Does the proposed measure potentially affect the establishment of, access to and functioning of R&D or innovation infrastructure?
- Could the measure add to or ease the administrative burden to test, pilot or demonstrate new goods, services and products?
- Could compliance costs and time for the development of innovative technologies/solutions be affected?

Does the measure affect the application of innovative solutions or help bring them to the market?

- Is the measure applied in an area with a relatively fast pace of innovation?
- Could the measure affect the introduction of future innovative solutions?
- Could the measure affect the innovation dynamics of specific markets?Could the measure add to or remove the administrative burden to bring new goods, services and products on the market?
- Will the proposed measure stimulate multi-disciplinary R&D?

Does the measure affect incentives around investment, growth, jobs or scaling up?

- Could the legislation change the innovation incentives and choices for R&D and innovation investments?
- Could the measure lead to a difference in innovation investment incentives in the EESC sub-region compared to third countries?
- Could the measure create or influence a preference for keeping firms at a size below a certain limit?
- Could the measure affect the incentives for companies to scale-up nationally or in the EESC sub-region?
- Will the proposed measure lead to societal innovation?

Source: UNECE, based on (European Commision, 2017).

The drive to make sure that regulations are aligned with the needs of IHGEs will take time to implement and is an on-going endeavour. In the short term, **the governments in the EESC sub-region may help the creation of an investment in potential IHGEs through temporary measures that enable potential IHGEs to benefit from as favourable a regulatory framework as possible** (while maintaining robust environmental standards and ethical principles). This can be done through consultative mechanisms that enable observations of enterprises driving transformative change to be considered (as was the case in Estonia for the development of sharing/platform economy business models, see box 2.3).

Promoting innovation through regulatory sandboxes

The increasing pace of change of technology and the emergence of new business models (platform economy, Fintech, etc.) requires new tools that strengthen policymakers' ability to anticipate change (e.g. foresight studies and horizon scanning); that enable innovators to propose changes to legislation or explore alternative modes of compliance; and foster the development of experimental approaches to regulation, aimed at testing new solutions or alternative business models before admitting them to the market (Simonelli & Renda, 2019).

Governments have increasingly taken steps to **create environments in which innovators can not only test the market viability but also the regulatory innovation required to introduce new products and services -** notably in the Fintech field (banking, insurance, securities) but also in other areas such as healthcare, mobility and energy[4].

Figure 2.10 · Lithuanian approach to Regulatory Sandboxes

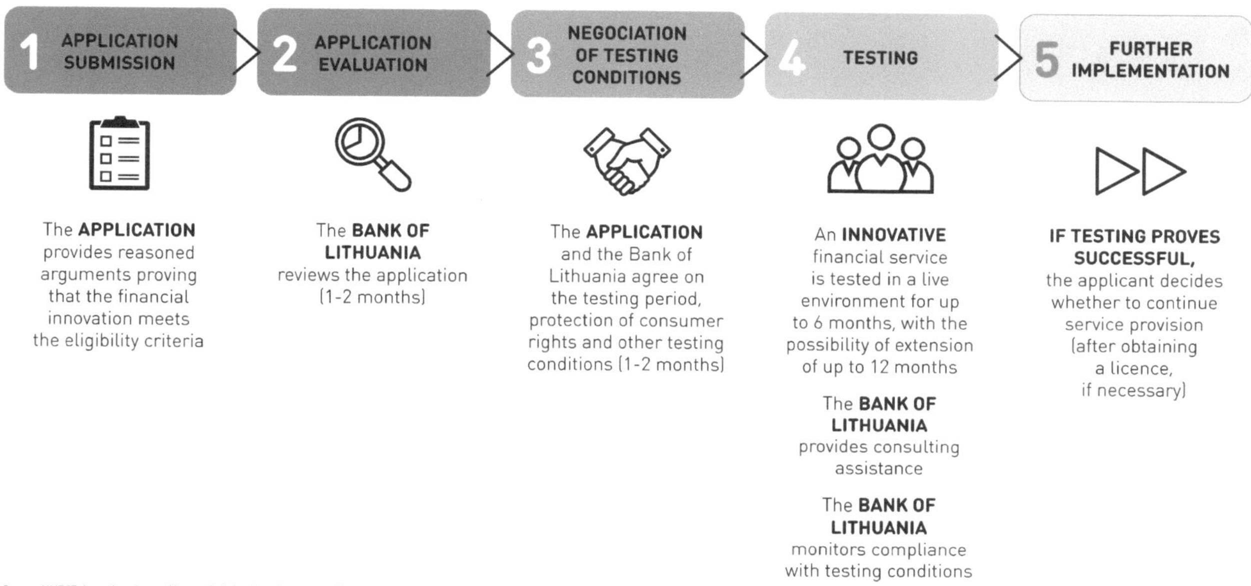

Source: UNECE, based on https://www.lb.lt/en/regulatory-sandbox

In Fintech, two main tools are used:

- ***Innovation hubs:*** These provide a means via which firms can engage with a public authority (supervisor) to raise questions and seek clarifications or non-binding guidance about Fintech-related issues in the context of compliance with the regulatory framework, licensing or registration requirements as well as any regulatory and supervisory expectations.
- ***Regulatory sandboxes:*** These go a step further and provide a special scheme in which companies can test innovative financial products, services or business models with actual customers in a controlled environment (a 'sandbox') pursuant to a specific testing plan agreed with the supervisor and subject to the application of distinct safeguards (Parenti, 2020).

Around 30 countries have experimented with regulatory sandbox-type approaches in the Fintech field and several of the EESC countries have Fintech companies already operating. For example, **Armenian-based PayX** aims to develop non-cash payments and

Box 2.5 Regulatory sandboxes as a tool for supporting IHGEs

As testbeds for innovation and regulation, regulatory sandboxes and similar environments offer a lot of potential wherever consumers, businesses and policymakers are facing major changes due to the digital transformation.

For example, regulatory sandboxes are indispensable in testing the role of autonomous, AI-assisted solutions for future transport and logistics systems as well as in the energy sector to trial innovative solutions for a future energy system increasingly based on highly digitized renewable energy and energy efficiency.

In Germany, the Economic Affairs Ministry has set up a large-scale regulatory sandbox entitled "Smart Energy Showcases – Digital Agenda for the Energy Transition" (SINTEG[a]), offering temporary spaces in which solutions for technical, economic and regulatory challenges relating to the energy transition can be developed and demonstrated.

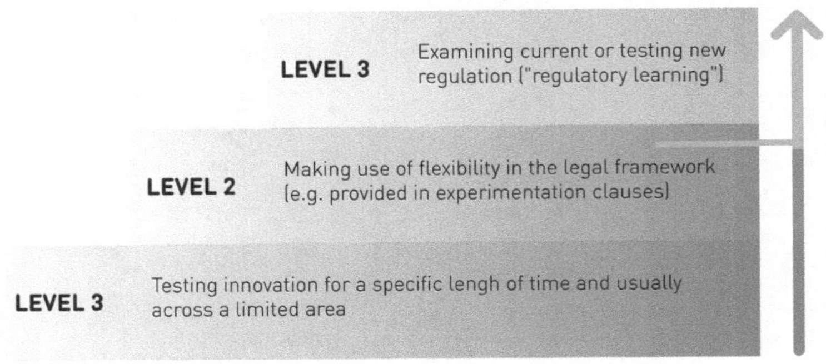

In the Fintech field, (Cornelli, 2020) found that entry into a regulatory sandbox is associated with **a higher probability of raising funding and an increase of on average 15 per cent in the funding raised**.

Regulatory sandboxes improve access to funding by reducing information asymmetries and regulatory costs for three reasons. First, the positive effect of sandbox entry on capital raised is particularly pronounced for smaller and younger firms which are usually subject to more severe informational frictions. Second, sandbox entry is followed by an increase in first-time investors and in the share of foreign investors. These investors are likely to face greater information asymmetries due to either geographical distance or a lack of previous relationships. Finally, CEOs without prior experience in financial regulation benefit more from the guidance provided by case officers during the process of obtaining authorization.

Source: UNECE, based on (BMWi, 2020) (Cornelli, 2020).
[a] See: https://www.sinteg.de/en/

online mobile payments using its own innovative solutions based on international best practices; while in **Georgia**, Fintech companies such as **Optio.Ai** have received support from GITA to develop AI-based applications for financial companies to categorize their customers' transactions and create conversational banking experiences that help people manage their finances. In addition, the National Bank of Georgia is a member of the Global Financial Innovation Network (GFIN) which supports cross-border testing of innovative financial products. The bank has set up its Financial Innovation Office to support effective communication between financial innovators and supervisors[5]. The **Ukrainian Association of FinTech and Innovation Companies**, founded in 2018, aims to foster the development of the domestic financial technology market, create a strong Fintech ecosystem and enhance financial inclusion. It currently has 59 members including Fintech companies, banks, microfinance companies and IT companies.

Countries such as Singapore have experimented with regulatory sandboxes in the health care field for early entrants into the telemedicine and mobile medicine space[6] while Portugal has established "Technological Free Zones" to foster cross-sector innovation (Box 2.6).

Box 2.6 Technological Free Zones in Portugal

In April 2020, the Portuguese Government unveiled plans for cross-sector "Technological Free Zones", as part of its Digital Action Plan to encourage experimentation in emerging technologies such as artificial intelligence, blockchains, 5G, nanotechnology, etc.

The zones will have tailored regulatory regimes that encourage innovation and experimentation and lessen the regulatory and legal burden on the developers of new and experimental technologies. The legal framework for the free zones goes beyond existing approaches to regulatory sandboxes which are typically set up for a specific sector or pre-defined area. The idea is to have a legal framework that promotes and streamlines experimentation activities in a cross-sector manner to take advantage of all the opportunities brought by innovative technologies..

Source: UNECE, based on https://eportugal.gov.pt/en/noticias.

Drawing on this experience, the opportunity to develop regulatory sandboxes and other testbed instruments could be explored by the EESC countries in areas including Fintech, AI applications for mobility, energy system transitions, etc. **The GFIN experience of piloting a cross-border sandbox to test financial innovations could be explored to create a larger market for testing new products and services across the EESC sub-region.**

An innovation friendly and pro-growth tax system

A key element of the business environment is an innovation friendly and pro-growth tax system. Two key issues are relevant in this respect for fostering IHGEs:

- Firstly, as potential IHGEs normally undertake more R&D and innovation than regular SMEs and are developing products and services in disruptive technologies, many will be young (start-up) firms for which targeted tax incentive schemes may be relevant.
- Secondly, the tax system may be geared to encourage investment by stimulating business angels and venture capitalists to invest in potential IHGEs. However, such incentives need to be carefully designed to avoid adverse effects and combined with other measures to develop an appropriate investment ecosystem.

Most countries providing R&D tax incentives focus the incentives on reducing the cost of R&D and encouraging increased expenditures on it. This approach can take various forms, including credits applied against income, reduced payroll taxes for wages and capital investments for R&D. It can also take the form of accelerated asset depreciation, allowing recovery of the initial investment faster than the prevailing economic depreciation of long-lived assets; or enhanced depreciation where taxpayers can recover more than 100 per cent of the cost of the R&D expenditures.

Two design features favour tax incentives. First, **tax incentives are often open-ended entitlements** which do not typically require annual spending authorization and are often unlimited in the amount of qualifying activity undertaken by a private company. Second, **tax incentives reduce the scope for discretionary selection of individual firms or projects** as they often do not have the pre-approval process or extensive reporting and audit requirements of most state-funding programmes (OECD, 2016)[7].

Box 2.7 Examples of tax incentives for young, innovative companies

In France, the young innovative company (*jeune entreprise innovante*) scheme[a] means that young firms (under 8 years old) carrying out R&D projects can benefit from a reduction in their taxation (exemption from corporate income tax (CIT) plus a reduction in capital gains tax) and exemption from social charges relating to highly qualified jobs such as engineers and researchers. In 2017, over 3700 firms benefitted from this scheme with a recent study identifying the scheme as having a significant positive effect on the growth of employment in young innovative firms, especially during their first two years.

In Belgium, the partial (80 per cent) withholding tax exemption scheme significantly contributes to the stimulation of private R&D investment, including for young innovative companies. As a result, an employer only has to transfer 20 per cent of the withholding tax owed to the tax authorities with the remaining 80 per cent staying with the employer as a direct cash benefit. By reducing the cost of employing skilled people (granted to R&D employees with a master's degree or higher), it provides an upfront incentive to invest in R&D and innovation.

(Mitchell, 2020) concluded that there is sufficient evidence to suggest that the range of tax credit schemes and incentives implemented by governments offer an attractive source of support for young and small companies and that many have gained significant benefits as a result. More specifically, there is some evidence of the larger effects of generic R&D tax measures on young firms, R&D intensity as well as country specific (e.g. in France) evidence of the positive effects of targeted R&D tax incentives on young firms' employment, productivity, sales and added-value.

Source: Author's analysis for UNECE, based on (Mitchell, 2020).
[a] See: https://www.enseignementsup-recherche.gouv.fr/cid5738/le-statut-de-la-jeune-entreprise-innovante-jei.html

None of the EESC countries currently have an R&D tax incentive scheme in place and only two allow for the deduction of R&D expenditure from corporate income tax (Table 2.5). In Ukraine, R&D expenses are deductible according to financial accounting rules and in Moldova, R&D expenses incurred during the fiscal year can be deducted as expenses. Belarusian enterprises tend to prefer reporting R&D expenses as current expenditures. Various other forms of incentives connected to high-tech or information technology companies also exist. However, they tend to be discretionary in the sense that they target companies either located in specific zones (e.g. high-tech parks) or operating within a particular sectoral categorization. The (OECD, 2020) noted that a lack of monitoring and evaluation of the impact of such tools makes it hard to evaluate the extent to which SMEs, as opposed to large companies, are benefitting from such broad-based incentives and increasing their innovation activities.

Belarus established the 'Hi-Tech Park' special regime based on applying Western law for companies registered in the park and is linked to giving them exemption from all

Table 2.5 Tax incentives relevant for IHGEs in EESC

Country	Tax incentives/deductions
Armenia	Since 2014, IT start-ups are exempt from paying corporate income tax (CIT) and a reduced income tax flat rate of 10 per cent is applied to employees. This measure is in effect until 2022[a]. Armenian resident companies implementing a business plan approved by the Government may deduct the amount of the annual salaries for the newly created jobs from the CIT liability of that year but not more than 30 per cent of the actual CIT calculated. The incentive is applicable for five fiscal years after the year the business starts.
Azerbaijan	Businesses operating in industrial and technology parks are eligible for certain privileges and exemptions for 10 years starting from the reporting year in which residents are registered in the industrial and technology park.
Belarus	Incentives to produce innovative, high-technology goods and laser-optical equipment on a list approved by Council of Ministers are exempt from CIT. Tax privileges are granted to residents of the High Technologies Park (HTP), however, some will be reduced or removed in 2021. The (OECD, 2020) notes that expenditure-based provisions in Belarus echo some good EU practices and make it possible to deduct R&D expenses from a company's profits with a multiplier of up to 1.5.
Georgia	Virtual zone person (a legal person engaged in IT activities and granted the status by the Government of Georgia): profit earned from supplying IT created by a virtual zone person outside Georgia is exempt from profit tax.
Moldova	Since 2017, a law on IT parks provides for tax incentives for the IT parks' residents that are active in certain activities (not only IT but also R&D in engineering, Biotech, etc.). The residents of the IT parks pay a simplified tax of 7 per cent of sales revenues.
Ukraine	R&D expenses are deductible according to financial accounting rules.

Source: UNECE, based on (PWc, 2017) and feedback on the handbook provided by EESC stakeholders.
[a] See: https://www.bdo.global/en-gb/microsites/tax-newsletters/world-wide-tax-news/issue-52-september-2019/armenia-tax-incentives-for-information-technology-startups-extended

corporate taxes, including VAT and profit tax as well as customs duties. This model has served as inspiration for similar arrangements existing or planned in other EESC countries including Azerbaijan, Moldova[8] and Georgia aimed at attracting both investors to invest in innovative local firms (primarily in IT field) and foreign direct investors to establish operations. However, **such schemes should be considered as transitory measures that help to foster an ecosystem for IHGEs pending an alignment of the overall business environment**.

Tax incentives for venture capital and business angels can play a role in fostering investment and are used across the EU and OECD countries. A 2017 study identified 18 desirable features in the design of venture capital and business angel tax incentives (PWc, 2017). Tax incentive design should use **qualifying criteria** (to limit the risk of tax avoidance) and promote investment quality via **performance-related tax relief** in combination with features that promote uptake. The positive here is that tax relief on future returns on investment will mean a greater focus on success by investors. In practice, tax incentives should be designed to incentivize investment in firms with high-growth characteristics rather than specific sectors (or businesses).

Box 2.8 Belarus High Technologies Park (HTP)

Initially created in 2005, the Belarus HTP had an initial focus on software development for clients using an outsourcing model. While the number of resident companies and exports they generated grew steadily over the next decade, the 2017 decree "On the Development of the Digital Economy" shifted the focus away from subcontracting to owning product-based businesses, generating a quantitative and qualitative leap in the number of companies and exports (from US$821 million in exports in 2016 to US$2.2 billion in 2019). Currently, the HTP hosts 969 residents with about 65,500 employees. The HTP residents produced almost a quarter of the nation's GDP growth in 2019 and generated considerable tax returns for the state budget.

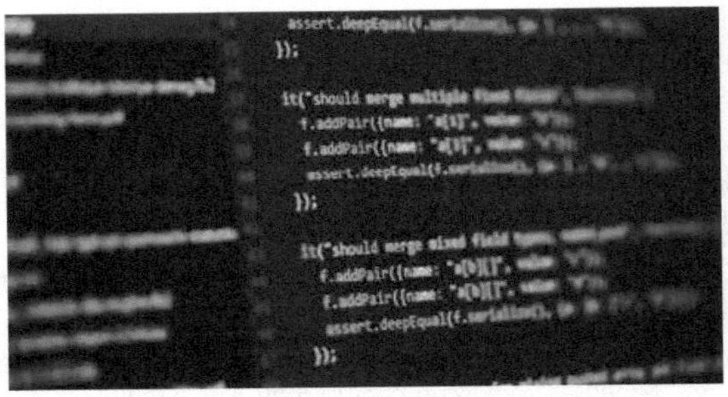

The HTP provides its residents with reduced taxes, a legal framework based on "English law", free movement of capital and transparent regulations for block chaining and cryptocurrencies. The following tax privileges are currently granted to HTP residents (some changes expected in 2021):

- Full exemption from CIT;
- Full exemption from VAT when selling goods, works, services, or property rights in Belarus;
- Full exemption from VAT and customs duties when importing certain goods for the purpose of using them in activities connected with high technology;
- No land tax is applicable to land plots situated in the HTP on which a construction project is being carried out, however, this exemption lasts no longer than three years;.
- Full exemption from real estate tax on buildings and installations, situated in the territory of the HTP;
- 9 per cent personal income tax for employees of residents of the HTP;
- No social insurance contributions on that part of employees' income exceeding the average salary in Belarus.

Source: UNECE, based on www.park.by.

The EESC countries should review their current use of tax incentives to encourage more entrepreneurial behaviour by both potential IHGEs and investors. Tax incentives alone will not sufficiently encourage IHGEs and should be part of a broader package of reforms and support; furthermore, they need to be carefully designed to avoid unwanted or undesirable effects.

Demand side policies - Government as a driver of innovation

The role of the Government in stimulating demand for innovative products and services is increasingly recognized as an important policy lever. Demand-side policies seek to increase the demand for innovation, improve conditions for the uptake of innovations and the diffusion of innovative technologies. **Demand-side innovation policies help stimulate innovation in areas where societal needs are pressing and where government action can complement market mechanisms, ideally with minimal financial outlays.** There is a range of policy instruments available in this regard, including setting standards that encourage innovation, providing incentives (tax, etc.) for the uptake of innovative technologies and notably, given the importance of the public budget in many countries, public procurement of innovative products and services.

Innovation-enhancing public procurement can be used to drive demand for innovation, providing opportunities to experiment in addressing social and economic challenges, as it has been demonstrated in the case of UNECE's work in Georgia[9] and showcased at the UNECE Teams of Specialists on Innovation and Competitiveness Policies[10]. It can also help foster potential IHGEs:

- *By creating demand for innovative products or services.* The ability to produce innovations often requires market opportunity (i.e. sufficient demand);
- *By helping IHGEs access private investment and funding.* The provision of a market through the awarding of a contract and positive evaluation by a public agency can help attract additional financing from private sources;
- *By helping IHGEs bridge the pre-commercialization gap for their innovative products and services by awarding contracts for pre-commercial innovations* (i.e. the first sales of technology). Pre-commercial contracts provide firms with the opportunity to enter the marketplace based on a successful application of their new products or services which can help reduce concerns about the perceived risk of adopting an innovative technology;
- *By assisting innovative firms to achieve the critical mass and competitiveness needed to bring prices down* which may be a key factor in the successful commercialization and adoption of an innovation.

There are two main public procurement type instruments that can be applied to support IHGEs to develop and test their innovative products:

1. ***Pre-Commercial Procurement (PCP)*** challenges industry from the demand side to develop innovative solutions for public sector needs and **provides a first customer reference that enables companies to create a competitive advantage in the market**.

2. ***Public Procurement of Innovation (PPI) solutions*** is procurement where **contracting authorities act as a launch customer for innovative goods or services which are not yet available** on a large-scale commercial basis and may include conformance testing.

The difference between the two types of approaches is illustrated in the following figure. PCP enables public procurers to compare alternative potential solution approaches and filter out the best solutions that the market can deliver to address the public need. PPI supplies an early reality check of specific public purchasing needs against workable solutions.

PPI is particularly useful in certain areas (e.g. mobility, health, construction, e-government, waste management, recycling) **where the public sector accounts for a large part of demand and can use procurement to address key societal challenges** in areas such as sustainable transport, resource-efficiency or health and aged care (European Commission, 2014). More recently, the PCP/PPI mechanisms have been used to support the public sector response to COVID-19 (European Commission , 2020). Among the six EESC countries, only Moldova has integrated innovation in public procurement through the introduction of innovation partnerships in the Law on Public Procurement (not in practice yet).

Figure 2.11 • Public procurement of innovative products and services

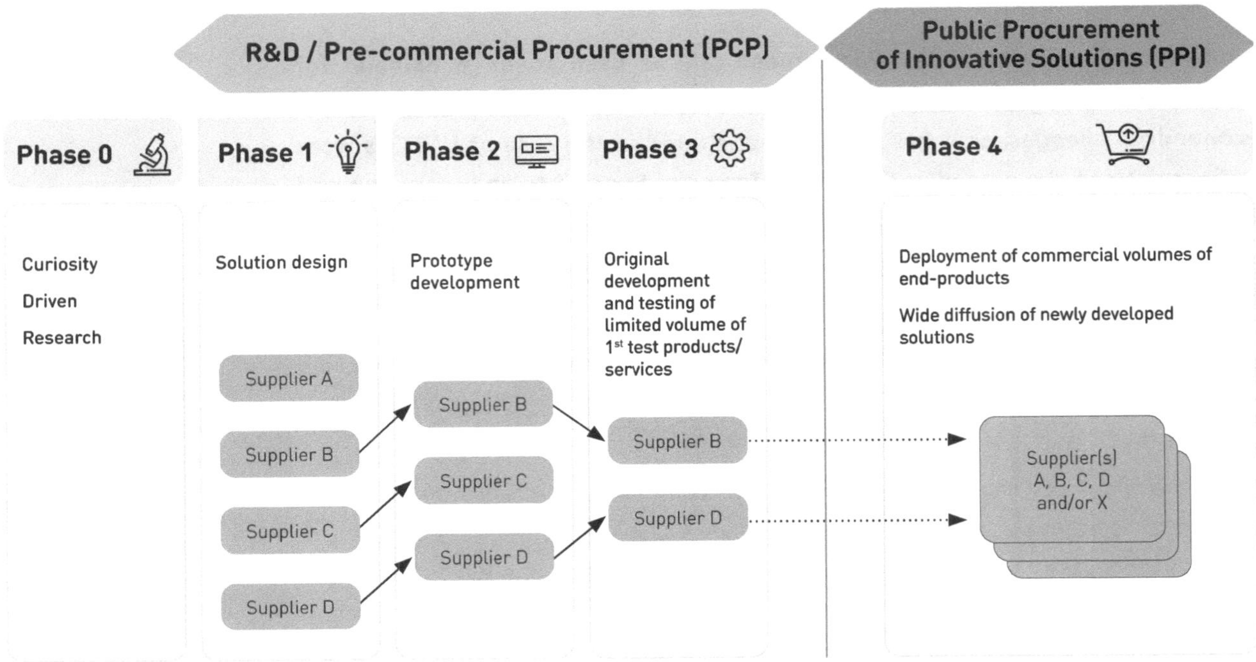

Source: UNECE, adapted from (European Commission, 2014).

When procurers represent a critical mass, they can create new lead markets by acting from the demand side so that entire sectors switch from proprietary to open standardized solutions and provide more flexible design solutions. Indeed, in certain sectors **the public-sector "demand pull" is an important factor in developing new markets for innovative solutions**[11].

In Austria, for example, an innovation platform has been established to provide a digital bridge between innovative companies and innovative public organizations (Box 2.9). Similar challenge-driven innovation initiatives exist in many European countries such as the CIVTech alliance[12] which help IHGEs develop and locally test solutions with global market potential. **IHGEs can benefit from being selected as suppliers to better anticipate demand for new solutions and shorten the time-to-market for their outputs**. Procurers can compare competing solutions and get a better price for an innovative solution that is more suited for the purpose at hand. In this way, public authorities may be able to steer the supply of innovative solutions from the demand side and leverage additional investment in R&D and innovation. **Harnessing the power of innovation from the EESC sub-region's public sector could help boost IHGE growth.**

2.2.2 Business development services for IHGEs

Standard business support and advisory services[13] **are, generally, not adapted to the needs of IHGEs which require a tailored package of support that can enable them to rapidly develop and deploy their innovative products and services**. This section distinguishes between three broad types of services:

- Advisory and mentoring services tailored to the growth stage needs of IHGEs;
- Developing "scale-up ecosystems" and peer-to-peer networks;
- Innovation support services (e.g. product development and testing, IPR).

The services and support required by potential IHGEs should be managed as part of a coordinated action targeted at a group of firms which meet a specific set of criteria or characteristics. This applies to business growth (scale-up) advisory services

Box 2.9 The IÖB innovation platform in Austria

In Austria, the innovation-promoting public procurement (IÖB) platform provides a marketplace where innovative companies can submit innovative solutions which are assessed by a panel of experts for their degree of innovation and applicability in the public sector. An IÖB-compatible label is awarded to positively assessed solutions.

Public sector bodies (ministries, agencies, regional and city authorities) open up their innovation processes and use the platform to launch challenges to which innovative companies can submit solutions. A jury selects the most interesting ideas and invites them to enter an "innovation dialogue" to test the solution.

For example, a recent challenge was launched by Autobahnen- und Schnellstraßen-Finanzierungs-Aktiengesellschaft (ASFINAG), a federal agency which plans, finances, builds, maintains, operates and collects tolls for 2200 kilometres of motorways and expressways. The current Austrian Government aims to increase national photo-voltaic generation capacity and ASFINAG would like to use the noise protection infrastructure for energy generation and contribute to CO2 reduction by offsetting polluting energy production. To achieve this, ASFINAG and potential suppliers must reconcile two goals in new facilities: the best possible noise protection and the highest levels of energy efficiency. The main question this challenge poses to would-be suppliers is «What is the best way to combine or integrate noise barriers and PV modules for highway use?»

Source: UNECE, based on https://www.ioeb.at/.

Figure 2.12 • Business development services for IHGEs

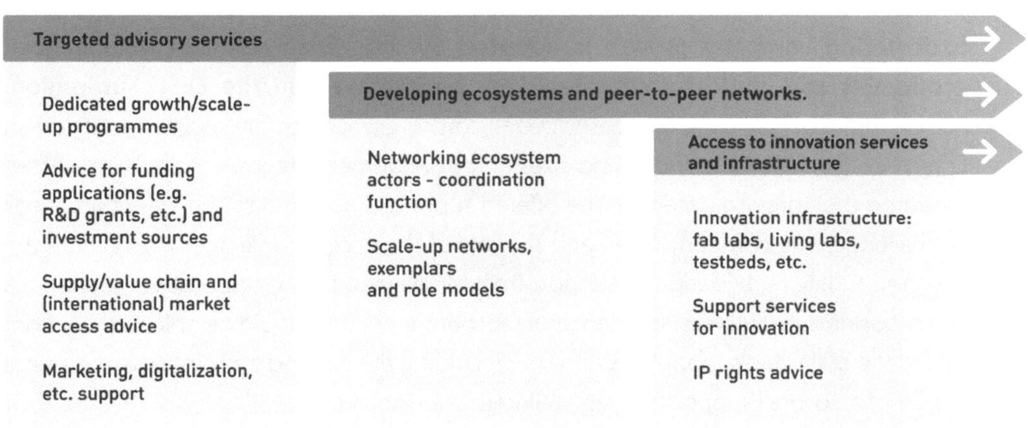

Source: UNECE

and dedicated programmes that are focused on growth and scaling (with a strong focus on international expansion) of a cohort of companies as well as an effort to develop entrepreneurial ecosystems in which growth ambitions can be realized.

A scale-up system should ideally include financial and investment players (*see the next section*) but also advisory services facilitating access to and use of the innovation infrastructure (testbeds, pilot plants, living labs, etc.) that enables IHGEs to develop and test their products and services, often through a user-driven or open innovation process. Indeed, according to (Hölzl, 2016): *"many of the innovation policies that target ambitious research projects at the firm level and foster the generation of differentiated knowledge bases will, in principle, also be effective for supporting high growth firms (HGFs), as long such policies are effectively embedded in the specific entrepreneurial ecosystem and do not simply foster incumbent R&D performers."*

The enterprise support frameworks in the EESC sub-region lack a high-growth component

All six EESC countries have put in place an enterprise (SME) development policy that covers the broad range of characteristics of SME and entrepreneurship (start-up) policies. The six countries have set up, or are developing, agencies to supply business development services (BDS) that enhance performance of firms. However, the focus of SME polices and agencies in the EESC sub-region is on technology start-ups and the standard BDS to the general population of SMEs with no targeting of IHGEs (Table 2.6). In addition, the research showed (OECD, 2020) that the SME support programmes in place require a more demand-driven and collaborative approach with the engagement of enterprises and the ecosystems' actors as well as thorough monitoring and evaluation mechanisms guided by specific key performance indicators (KPIs) which are lacking.

A first step for all six EESC countries towards enhancing support for IHGEs through services should be to draw up **a focused strategy that distinguishes between standard BDSs provided to all SMEs and customised BDSs targeted at *potential IHGEs* provided via a client management or portfolio-type approach** (Table 2.7). As ambitious firms target geographically broader markets and as export-oriented entrepreneurs tend to have greater growth ambitions, the services should include support for market access (see section 2.2.5).

The account management system which allows for a more personalized approach to fostering company growth is adopted by enterprise agencies in advanced economies and could be considered by policymakers in the EESC sub-region. For example, on an on-going basis, 2000 Scottish companies are assisted by Scottish Enterprise (SE). They are of differing sizes and development stages, but each is selected based on their growth potential. The offered support is adjusted to the identified needs or challenges the company faces, and the role of the account manager is to ensure the easy and timely mobilization of support from all relevant public or private organizations in the business growth system. Hence, an account manager should be able to draw from a portfolio of flexible support mechanisms, including the existing ones that may be useful as part of an overall support package tailored to an individual IHGE.

An example of a **scale-up programme based on working with a cohort of potential IHGEs** is the Enterprise Singapore Scale-up SG initiative (Figure 2.13).

Table 2.6 Enterprise support framework in the EESC sub-region

Country	Enterprise support agencies	Current policy framework	Policy initiatives oriented towards IHGEs
Armenia	Investment Support Center[a]	Small and medium-sized entrepreneurship development strategy 2020-2024 (adopted in 2020)	**No specific policy measures in favour of IHGEs** – focus on IT/software fields. The new Ministry of High-Tech Industry also provides grants for "ideas to business" projects.
Azerbaijan	Small and Medium Business Development Agency (SMDA)[b]	SMDA established in 2018 2016 SME Strategic Roadmap until 2020	**No specific policy measures supporting IHGEs** – however, the strategy focuses, among other priority areas, on the promotion of SME innovation[c]. Growing emphasis on the need to diversify away from the oil and gas sectors (e.g. the ICT sector) with support from the National Innovation Agency (created in 2019).
Belarus	The establishment of an SME agency is planned	SME Development Strategy 2030	**No specific policy measures supporting IHGEs** – but SME innovation is in focus. 2020 OECD report on business development services and high-growth enterprises in Belarus laid out the state-of-the-art in IHGE development and provided recommendations.
Georgia	Enterprise Georgia[d] Georgian Innovation and Technology Agency[e]	SME Development Strategy 2016-2020	**No specific policy measures supporting IHGEs** - but the strategy contains objectives on SME innovation and R&D[f]. It is GITA rather than Enterprise Georgia that focuses on developing an entrepreneurial innovation ecosystem and high-potential start-ups.
Moldova	Organization for Small and Medium Enterprises Sector Development[g]	SME Development Strategy 2012-2022	**No specific policy measures supporting IHGEs** – aside from the IT park-style support.
Ukraine	SME Development Office[h] under the Ministry of Economic Development, Trade and Agriculture	SME Development Strategy ran until 2020	**No specific policy measures supporting IHGEs** – but the strategy emphasizes developing the innovation potential of SMEs, including through the Ukrainian Start-up Fund (already in place)

Source: Author's analysis for UNECE.

[a] See: https://www.isc.am/

[b] https://smb.gov.az/

[c] Azerbaijan-Driving-Diversification-through-Strengthened-Entrepreneurship.pdf (oecd.org)

[d] http://www.enterprisegeorgia.gov.ge/en/home

[e] https://gita.gov.ge/eng

[f] Monitoring-Georgia's-SME-Development-Strategy-2016-2020.pdf (oecd.org)

[g] https://odimm.md/en

[h] https://sme.gov.ua/sme-development-office/

Table 2.7 Key building blocks of a portfolio/client management system for IHGEs

Building block	Description
Dedicated high-growth units or teams	Depending on the baseline situation in each country, the support unit (the high-growth team) can be based in an existing SME agency or within a dedicated stand-alone organization. The people acting as account managers should ideally have prior business experience (e.g. as an SME manager or start-up founder) to ensure their credibility.
Selection/segmentation criteria	Based on a mix of objective criteria, "trigger points" (e.g. management change, product/service offering) and outreach to determine the level of growth ambition of companies. Typically, this will not be based on the sectoral or technological fields in which companies operate but the companies will usually be selected based on an introductory diagnostic step (that will include collecting data on company performance, analysing business strategy, product portfolio, etc.) which can be conducted either by qualified agency staff or experienced business consultants accredited by the agency to carry out the diagnostic.
Support adjusted to each stage of growth and the type of company	The type of advice and support required by a manufacturing firm growing after a change of management or new product development will be different from that of a technology start-up that needs to secure investment and scale rapidly on international markets. A support programme where potential IHGEs work together over a period of time accompanied (mentored) by a cohort of their peers and guided by highly experienced entrepreneurs can help foster network-based forms of support and experiential learning (see Singaporean case below).
Inter-agency co-operation and partnership with private sector expertise	The delivery of advice and services to potential high-growth firms is best done via a network of accredited experts (finance, management, etc.) rather than a single agency or organization. Business owners will often place more faith in advice by mentors who are successful entrepreneurs, investors or specialists (legal, intellectual property, branding, etc.) in their field. The account manager's role is to help steer the growth process and make sure the right advice is proffered at the right time.

Source: Author's analysis for UNECE.

Box 2.10 Account management of growth companies: the Scottish Enterprise example

The aim of account management is to produce economic impacts by helping supported companies achieve growth aspirations, generate and safeguard employment as well as improve efficiency and productivity. The account management process is facilitated by an account manager (AM) – a single point of contact who coordinates one-to-one support, advice and guidance to a strategic contact(s) within the supported company.

The AM has access to a team of specialists (within SE and through external consultants) who provide intensive input across key areas regarding business growth, including how to gain access to finance and investment, innovation, market development, business improvement as well as organizational and strategy development.

Bespoke support is provided for agreed growth projects, as articulated in the Company Review Workbook (CRW), a diagnostic tool, that aims to deliver additional growth and demonstrate a clear rationale for SE intervention. The CRW is a tool used by AMs to aid the understanding of the company and its growth ambitions and supports AMs to realize this ambition. The CRW contains a company profile, key performance metrics, forecasts and growth ambitions as well as outlining the specific development projects which the company will undertake to realize its growth ambitions.

Source: UNECE, based on (Upperquartile , 2013).

Table 2.8 The impact of targeted services for companies with growth potential – two recent examples involving Scottish Enterprise involvement

Launching an Innovative Product	Managing Rapid Growth
The company: A technology company looking for external funding to launch an innovative and wearable unique sports performance device.	**The company:** A company which has been manufacturing candles since 2010 and sells candle making supplies online since 2013.
The challenge: Resourcing the company, creating a supply chain and securing the funding to launch the product.	**The challenge:** Rapid growth in sales has placed a strain on the company in several areas, e.g. lack of knowledge/experience in growth areas; e-commerce site does not support additional currencies/languages and customer support calls are a significant drain on staff time with no clear systems and procedures.
SE Support: The company received a wide range of support and benefited from a wider Account Team approach. As part of this, they received an R&D grant to develop their product. The Scottish Enterprise's High Growth Ventures team offered support to validate offering/market, secure seed funding and identify non-executive directors. The company received specialist advice from one of the High Growth Venture advisers on developing the supply chain, routes to international markets, how to develop a business strategy, revenue model, digital marketing and made connections with potential non-executive directors as well as in the Globalscot network. The Scottish Investment Bank has been a key investor and supporter of the company, participating in every funding round to date.	**SE Support:** The SE account team engaged with the company to help them scale-up. Support included technical leadership and expertise (Fulfilment & Production Manager), systems and management information (a company appointed accountancy firm to manage accounts), executive education (owners attended the Entrepreneurial Development Programme at the Massachusetts Institute of Technology) and the implementation of a customer service training scheme.
Impact: The company secured over GBP 3.6 million in equity investments and GBP 350,000+ sales across 35 countries worldwide. They have created a manufacturing supply chain, predominately based in Scotland.	**Impact:** Based on the roadmap for growth, the business sought to double its turnover from GBP £1.3 million in 2015-2016 to GBP 3.1 million in 2018-2019 with staff numbers growing from 10 to 26 employees over the same period. The company's five-year ambition is GBP 8 million in turnover of which GBP 5 million coming from e-commerce.

Source: UNECE, based on (Scottish Enterprise, 2018).

Figure 2.13 • Singapore Scale-up SG programme method

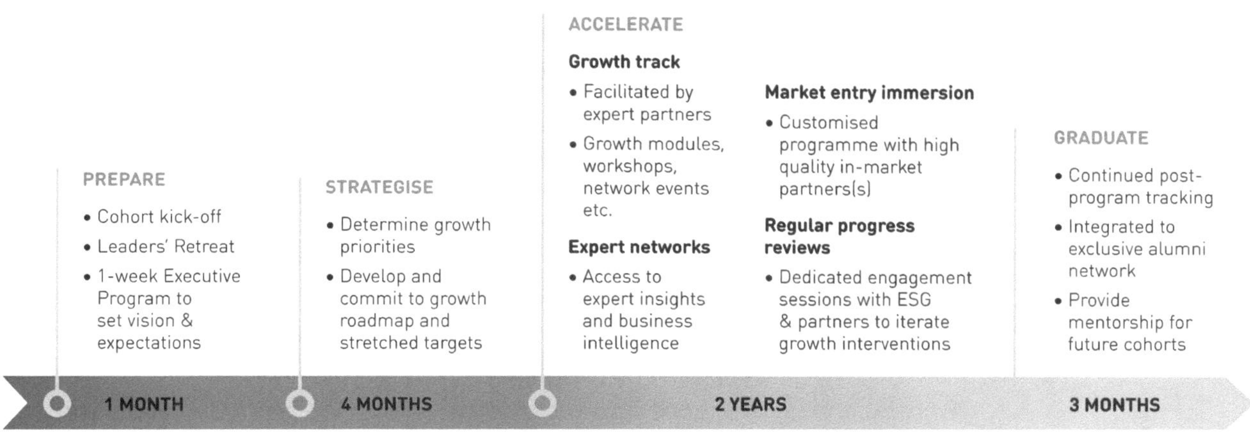

Source: UNECE, adapted from https://www.enterprisesg.gov.sg/non-financial-assistance/for-singapore-companies/growth-partnership-programme/scale-up-sg

Participating companies go through the programme in cohorts aimed at facilitating peer networks, collaboration and learning. Each cohort comprises 10 to 15 companies with similar growth profiles and priorities with each cycle lasting 2.5 years and comprised of four key phases. A co-funding principle applies to ensure commitment from companies participating in the programme. Up to 70 per cent of the programme's participation costs are paid by Enterprise Singapore.

The inaugural run of the programme brought together 25 firms in two cohorts – the first one featuring the firms from the lifestyle and consumer goods field, a manufacturing and engineering cluster as well as trade and connectivity (e.g. food distribution and leasing of industrial vehicles); while the second cohort comprised firms from the lifestyle and consumer goods field, trade and connectivity as well as urban solutions. The range of fields where the companies are active underlines the fact that potential IHGEs firms are not restricted to a few high-tech niches, but also involve food manufacturing, fuel distribution, bathroom supplies, restaurants and catering, etc.

In the EESC sub-region, a pilot growth/scale-up programme could potentially be run at the multi-country level (e.g. with support from the EU and/or another international funding institution) **with a group of 4-5 potential IHGEs selected per country for mentoring and support**. The advantage would be in companies building international partnerships to grow their business in the region and beyond enabling them to then serve as mentors to future cohorts of participating companies.

An ecosystem conducive to high growth entrepreneurial activity

In the early 2000s, countries placed a lot of emphasis on SME and entrepreneurship policies to develop start-up ecosystems. This has helped generate a significant entrepreneurial dynamic but has not always paid off in terms of the start-up's growth neither nationally, nor internationally. As (Isenberg, 2012) wrote: *"If we look at entrepreneurship in terms of extraordinary value creation and capture, ... then it is clear that value can be created and captured in a large variety of ways, and there is no a priori reason to think doing this from scratch via a start-up is the only or even the best way. Extraordinary value creation may involve acquiring, re-purposing, spinning off, or recombining underutilized or undervalued assets."*

Since the mid-2010s, many countries have been paying **increasing attention has been paid in many countries to the need to extend these efforts into developing entrepreneurial ecosystems that foster scale-ups via coordinated efforts to support sustained growth of both start-ups and existing SMEs.**

A scale-up ecosystem needs to include the right mix of elements to support value creation and growth over time and that works for all types of firms (Figure 2.14). Many of the elements exist already and the issue is to incentivize and mobilize them to focus on the growth potential of IHGEs.

Fostering a high-growth or scale-up ecosystem does not necessarily require large public investments. It means putting in place a team or partnership that coordinates the efforts of existing ecosystem players and communicates clearly the needs and challenges of IHGEs while helping to channel support to fulfil their growth potential. Daniel Isenberg has rightly stated *"What matters is that more and more companies grow more and more rapidly; not all companies, that would be impossible, but a hard core, a critical mass. Nor do they necessarily all need to become big: what is important is that more and more companies are moving dynamically upward".*[14]

Figure 2.14 · Components of a scale-up ecosystem

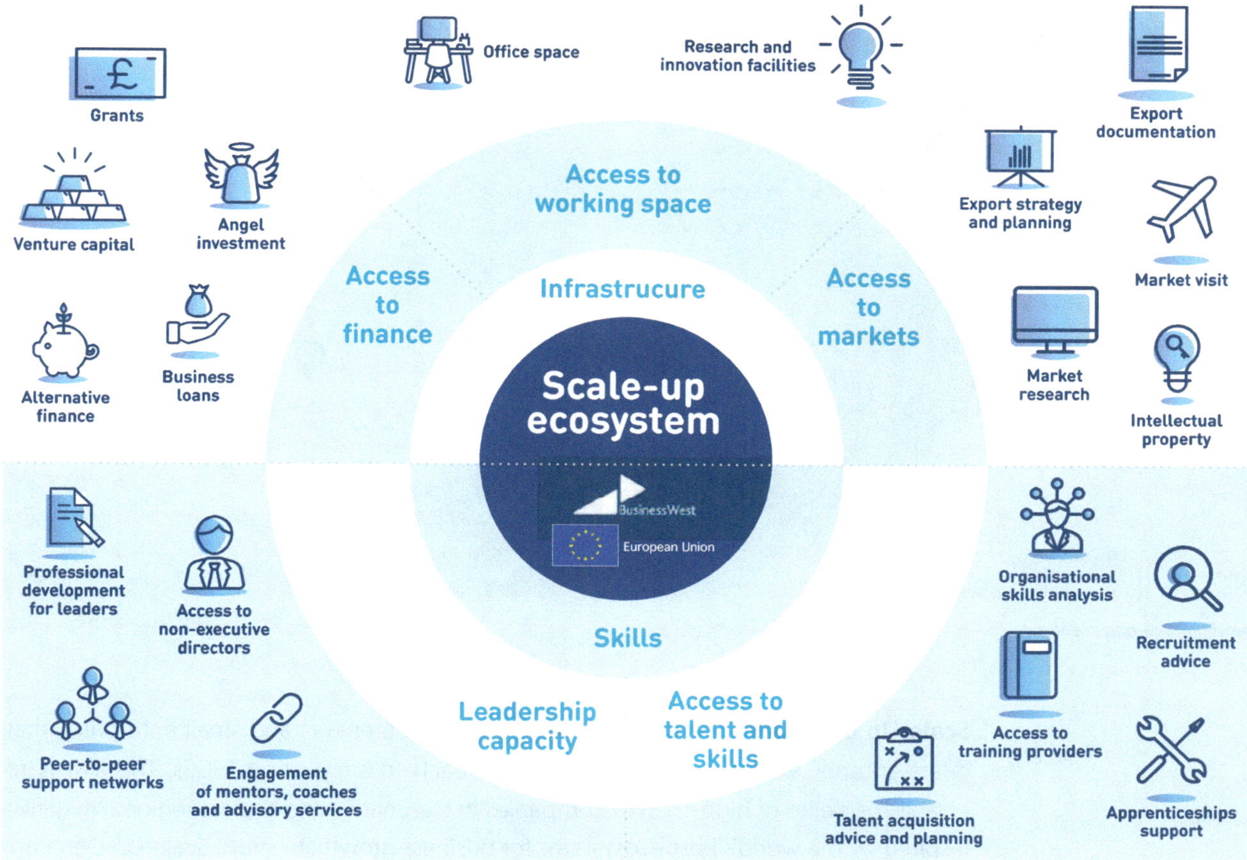

Source: UNECE, adapted from https://www.businesswest.co.uk.

Various examples of public-private partnerships working to develop scale-up ecosystems exist and these can serve as pointers for reinforcing the support to IHGEs in the EESC sub-region. For example, the **UK the ScaleUp Institute** – a private sector and not-for-profit company – works to improve the ecosystem for scale-ups. The Institute collaborates with policymakers, corporate partners and educational establishments to map the support for scale-ups, analyse trends and promote success stories that can serve as role models for other companies[15]. Across the UK, a network of enterprise and development agencies help to coordinate and structure their local ecosystems. In the West of England, the Scale up Generator promotes the support community and opportunities that exists for fast-growing companies (Figure 2.15). The initiative notably aims to:

- To invigorate the investment ecosystem in the region and improve access to finance via a Quarterly Investment Briefing and an 'Investor In Residence' service;
- To encourage founders and aspiring scale-ups by sharing inspiration through scale-up briefing events, a growing body of case studies and peer-to-peer networks;
- To build the profile of the region as a home for successful scale-up companies by providing resources, data and maps to promote scale-ups and by sharing information to minimize duplication, maximize collaboration and make support more accessible.

Figure 2.15 · Scale-up ecosystem map for West of England

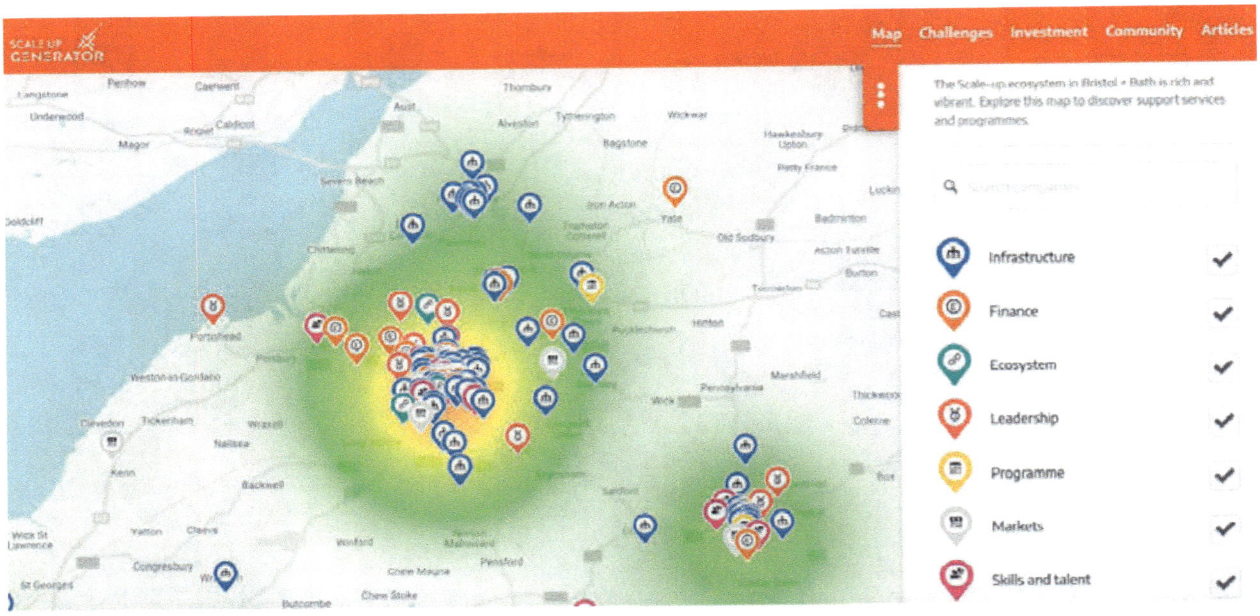

Source: https://www.scaleupgenerator.co.uk .

Scale-Up Denmark[16] is a training concept for entrepreneurs and small enterprises that offers another example of a structured approach to supporting IHGEs. The aim is to establish an elite of high-growth companies in Denmark using a cross-regional initiative inspired by the world's best ecosystems for business growth. In short, Scale-Up Denmark seeks to:

- Attract high performing enterprises – both Danish and international
- Provide access to seed and venture capital;
- Engage market-leading firms from the regional ecosystem;
- Involve leading universities, research institutions and science parks;
- Provide an easy access to the services of the entire Danish business support system.

Selected companies receive a customized accelerator programme in cooperation with industry leaders, investment managers and industry professionals – resulting in a high-growth business plan.

At the European level, the **Scaleup4Europe project**[17] has established four cross-border "Scaleup Labs" based on the living lab concept to support qualifying scale-ups in achieving a "proof of scalability". The proof of scalability is achieved when the scale-ups comply with all requirements of general technological, market, organizational and investor readiness as well as their innovation being adapted to a specific customer need. The overall goal is to establish sustainable support structures that connect "deep tech" communities in four countries in an innovative way creating a lasting and larger regional scale-up support system[18].

Such examples offer **pointers to policymakers in the EESC sub-region on means and instruments to refocus and strengthen their existing start-up ecosystems** to provide more targeted support to IHGEs. Four main steps to do this can be identified:

1. *Identify enterprises with potential for growth* (e.g. using data relevant for trigger points such as recent investments or changes of ownership) as well as mapping existing high-growth firms and scale-ups that serve as role models of successful growth strategies in diverse types of companies and sectors.
2. *Map the existing support* that is available to potential IHGEs *and identify gaps in the ecosystem* in terms of the main challenges faced by such firms (e.g. through business surveys, information collected in cooperation with chambers of commerce, clusters associations or accelerators).
3. *Internationally promote and network the group of potential IHGEs* and the advantages of the national business growth system through public-private partnerships (e.g. a task force) between government agencies (e.g. inward investment and export services) and high-growth business support organizations and investors.
4. *Monitor and evaluate the performance of enterprises that have been supported* (e.g. compared to the performance of a control group to measure additionality) and assess how to improve performance or fill gaps in the ecosystem over time.

Access for IHGEs to innovation services and infrastructure

A key part of a high-growth ecosystem is the availability of quality research and innovation (R&I) infrastructure and specialized engineering, technology and testing services to support the design and development of innovative products and services by IHGEs. The EESC countries and their R&I systems are still in a process of restructuring, with a significant need for increased investment in science and removal of barriers to successfully exploit existing research specializations. Innovation policies in the EESC sub-region are currently too narrowly focused on research and tech start-ups. **While the institutional frameworks for designing and implementing innovation policy are evolving, they remain insufficient to effectively support a broader based uptake of innovation methods and processes in the sub-region's national economies** (UNECE, 2020).

In the context of exploiting R&D results, a well-functioning and balanced IP rights system is a means of encouraging R&D and innovation activities by potential IHGEs. Despite the relatively good performance of the IP rights framework (World Economic Forum, 2019), the EESC countries have ample room for improvement in this area, in particular on enhancing the skills of the judiciary handling IP rights cases (OECD, 2020). This would increase the likelihood of international investors licensing technology to companies in the EESC sub-region (e.g. easily imitable technologies such as software) and can thus improve the chance of attracting equity investments. In addition, raising awareness and developing skills of potential entrepreneurs on the importance of IP rights as a tool to ensure the success of the innovative idea and its further growth as a part of a thriving business is also crucial for IHGEs development.

In short, due to the relatively weak research systems and insufficiently developed research commercialization and technology licensing frameworks, interviewees from the EESC sub-region were generally sceptical about the potential of an "R&D commercialization route" (research spin-offs, etc.) for local IHGEs**.** However, in some niche areas that build on traditionally strong science fields such as mathematics, the potential for supporting the emergence of IHGEs based on new technologies is viewed as more promising (e.g. artificial intelligence).

Table 2.9 Innovation infrastructure and services for IHGEs in the EESC sub-region

Country	Illustrative example of innovation infrastructure and services
Armenia	Armenia has a **relatively developed** innovation infrastructure, notably **focused on IT and engineering**, including technology parks and investments by foreign multinationals (Microsoft, National Instruments, Nokia, etc.) into industrial research and training labs, e.g. the Armenian National Engineering Laboratories at the National Polytechnic University. The **Engineering City project**[a] is a public-private partnership between the Government of Armenia and a consortium of private companies. The initiative, located in Yerevan, aims to develop an environment for high-tech engineering companies with the purpose of facilitating and accelerating the development of complex engineering solutions. It provides a full range of *advanced equipment, research and prototyping labs, machine tooling and production facilities* that are accessible to all the high-tech engineering residents (that use measurement equipment, prototyping labs and machine tooling during the development and production of their products and solutions). The **Enterprise Incubator Foundation**, founded in 2002, is one of the largest technology business incubators in IT and high-tech development agencies in the region. The foundation is based in the Engineering City and the programmes implemented by it are aimed at developing the ICT and high-tech sectors in Armenia.
Azerbaijan	The innovation infrastructure in Azerbaijan remains **limited** to a few industrial and high-technology parks which offer space and physical infrastructure but generally offer no or limited technical and business services to residents (UNECE, 2020). Support for developing an innovative ecosystem is part of the mandate of the **Innovation Agency**'s Support & Acceleration department which is responsible for designing and implementing programmes through the **Barama Innovation and Entrepreneurship Centre**[b]. The centre was the first business incubator in Azerbaijan, created with the support of Azercell Telecom LLC and PASHA Bank in 2009. The centre's main goal is **to grow the digital ecosystem** in Azerbaijan. The centre includes an innovation laboratory, business incubator and offers entrepreneurship support, business solutions and partnership areas. The centre's services include support for *Pre/Acceleration* (a 3-month intensive programme for business/product development), support to launch products, *mentorship expertise* from 50+ local and international mentors and *network connections* to key ecosystem players.
Belarus	The innovation infrastructure in Belarus has been actively developing in recent years, including the establishment of 16 technology parks and 8 technology transfer centres. However, many are still in **the initial stages of development**, limiting their activity to leasing premises and equipment and in need of significant further investment and training for staff. One exception is **EnCata (Engineering Catalyst)**[c], which provides end-to-end engineering services to help its customers complete the journey from a good idea through to design and development before advancing to mass-production and market launch. It runs *a design engineering and manufacturing centre in Minsk* and is the *first private Technopark in Belarus*. Based on their experience, EnCata realized the importance of a maker space for deep tech and hardware start-ups so they launched the MAKEIT CENTER[d], located adjacent to their design and manufacturing facilities so residents could build their own mock-ups and proof of concept prototypes. This fablab is part of the engineering ecosystem, allowing promising young companies to develop their ideas in a fast and cost-efficient way.
Georgia	Since 2016, Georgia's **Innovation & Technology Agency** has been developing innovation infrastructure via the network of three tech parks, two innovation centres and 22 fablabs (maker-spaces) across the country. Start-ups or interested individuals benefit from the free of charge access to co-working spaces, training and high-tech equipment which helps mature their ideas into specific products and develop hardware products using the high-tech equipment. GITA's overall goal is to foster a technology and innovation ecosystem for innovative individuals and enterprises.

Table 2.9 Innovation infrastructure and services for IHGEs in the EESC sub-region (Concluded)

Country	Illustrative example of innovation infrastructure and services
Moldova	Moldova's existing public innovation infrastructure is rather **limited** (one tech park with limited value-added services) (UNECE, 2020) and the legal framework governing science and technology parks which allows for the establishment of innovation infrastructure facilities by public entities, associations and clusters was only adopted in 2018. However, there are privately run innovation spaces that provide co-working spaces, organize hackathons, etc. For example, **Tekwill**[e], located at the Technical University of Moldova is a 4,000m^2 hub that provides facilities and services for start-ups and growth firms that range from co-working spaces and tech labs (IoT, 3D printing) to tech community events. In 2018, **FabLab Chisinau** (occupying 700 m^2) was launched in addition to Tekwill with small-scale prototyping and production workshops equipped with state-of-the-art, computer-assisted equipment and machinery.
Ukraine	Partly due to its relative scale, Ukraine has a **vast array of innovation infrastructure** elements, including 26 science parks, 16 technology parks and 22 innovation centres. The extent to which such infrastructure investment has fostered IHGEs is not clear and many of the organizations are not currently operational due to funding issues. The private sector is also investing in facilities for lab work, co-working and prototyping as well as mentoring services and the like which can support IHGEs. The **UNIT.City innovation park**[f] in Kyiv brings together three accelerators running eight programmes and 10 state-of-the-art laboratories such as the FabLab Fabricator, Sensorama VR/AR Lab and a Blockchain Lab as well as a coding school.

Source: UNECE, based on (UNECE, 2020).
[a] http://engineeringcity.am
[b] https://barama.az/
[c] https://encata.net/about-encata
[d] https://makeit.center/en
[e] https://www.tekwill.md/about
[f] https://unit.city/en/home/

One key take-away from this is that **the EESC countries should balance investment in innovation infrastructure (prototyping facilities, industrial R&D labs, pilot plants, etc.) with funding for value-added services (including ideation, proof of concept, testing and piloting, living labs, etc.) that provide support to IHGEs to engage in the development of market ready products and services.**

2.2.3. Finance and investment services adapted to growth stages

The type, number of rounds and scale of investment required by IHGEs differs markedly from the financing required by standard SMEs. The different growth phases (Figure 2.16) of an IHGE will mobilize financial instruments ranging from family and friends, crowdfunding[19] and business angels[20] through to government subsidies (grant, loans as well as tax incentives) and equity investments. Beyond interventions to tackle market and system failures that restrict access to finance, a key role for public policy in this respect is to **foster the development of an investor ecosystem** that ensures potential IHGEs have access to the finance they require. This can include co-investing, supporting financial education and public-private partnerships in the finance field, etc.

Figure 2.16 • Finance stages for high-growth firms

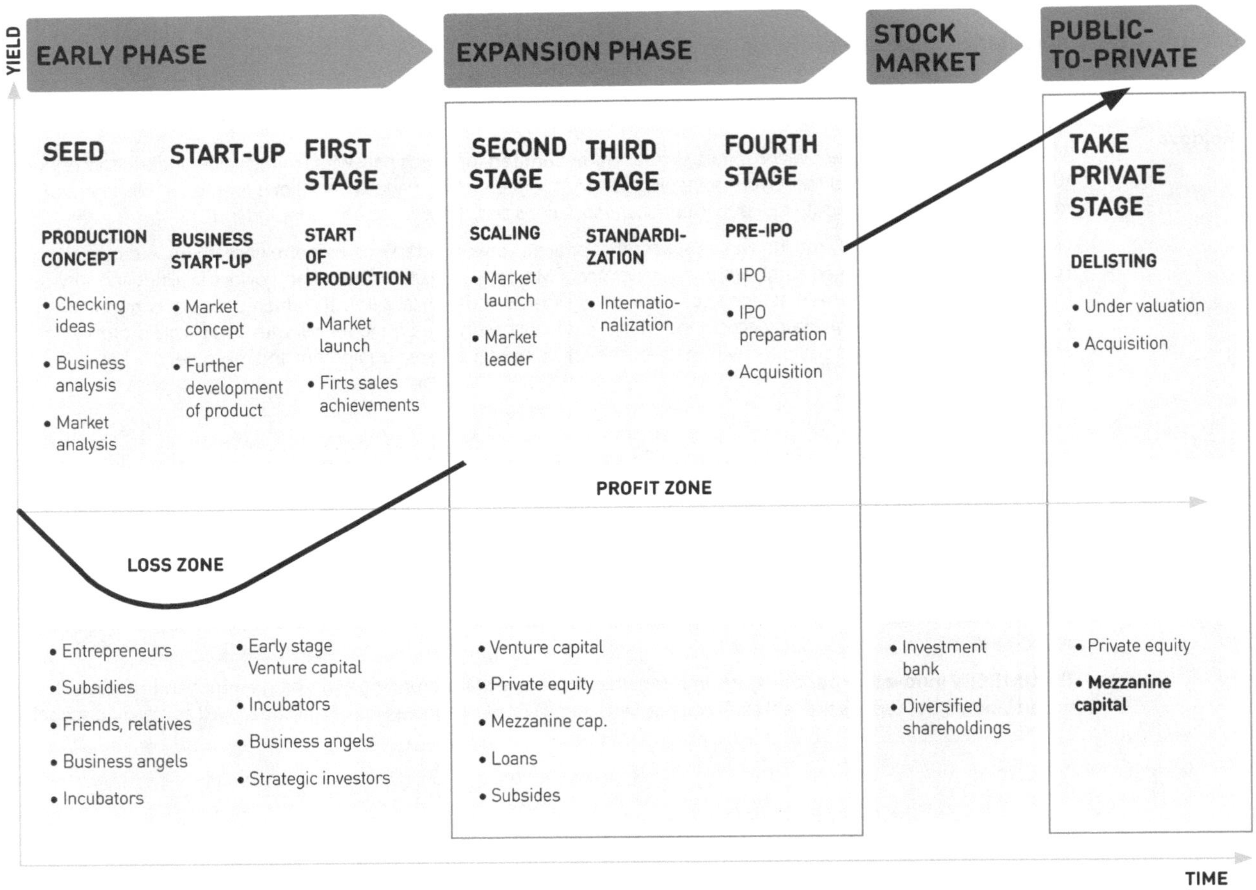

Source: UNECE, adapted from (Wilson, 2015).

Debt financing

Access to finance, adapted to the need of diverse types of businesses at different stages in their development, is generally considered as a, if not the, critical factor for sustaining successful growth. **While commercial bank lending is not best suited to the needs of fast-growing innovative firms, its availability does provide an indication of the sophistication of the financial system and likelihood of IHGEs securing at least part of their funding from domestic sources** (e.g. banks loans with public sector credit guarantees can be used during the expansion phase). **The financial sector in the EESC sub-region is insufficiently developed and remains a major obstacle for business development** (OECD, 2020): domestic credit provided by banks throughout the sub-region averages 35 per cent of GDP compared to 85 per cent in the EU and an average of approximately 80 per cent for all OECD countries. However, the situation varies significantly from one EESC country to another.

Access to credit (credit information systems, collateral and bankruptcy laws) is most complicated in Belarus (ranked 104th globally in the World Bank's Doing Business index 2020), with Azerbaijan ranking highest among EESC countries on this indicator; but access to finance remaining a significant barrier to SME growth[21] while Armenia and Georgia have the most favourable situation in terms of bank lending given their steady rate credit growth. Hence, Governments in the region, with international donor and financial institutions support, have developed credit guarantee schemes to improve access for firms (including start-ups such as in Armenia via the Investment Support Centre agency[22]) to bank finance.

An example of efficient debt financing for IHGEs can be found in Estonia's KredEx loan instruments which is briefly detailed below in Box 2.11.

Box 2.11 Loan instruments tailored to different stage of growth – KREDEX Estonia

KredEx is a public sector financial institution that helps Estonian companies to develop faster and expand securely into foreign markets. To do so, KredEx offers loans, venture capital, credit insurance and guarantees assured by the state. Amongst the portfolio of support, it provides two loan instruments which are relevant for IHGEs.

Start-up loan of up to €100,000

A KredEx start-up loan is intended for financing investments and circulating capital in start-ups and companies that have been operating for up to three years. It helps companies that struggle with a lack of capital and have insufficient sureties or operating history to secure a bank loan to start operations. The maximum amount of the start-up loan is €100,000, of which up to €50,000 may be used for the financing of circulating capital. Compared to a standard bank loan, a company is required to have less collateral and generally the personal surety of the sole proprietor of the loan recipient is sufficient. This obligation of surety for the loan is 25 per cent of the total borrowed, on the condition that the company uses the start-up loan in accordance with its intended purpose.

Capital loan – a subordinated loan of up to €2 million

A capital loan is a subordinated loan aimed at companies that have proven the operability of their business model and are planning to make investments in development as well as their volume of operations. It is of assistance if a company wishes to finance its rapid growth with a loan but its self-financing level is too low to receive a bank loan or it lacks sufficient sureties. KredEx places capital at the disposal of such a company which, thanks to subordination, raises the company's self-financing level in the eyes of other financiers. This, in turn, creates the opportunity to secure additional funding, for example, a bank loan. The amount of a capital loan is from €100,000 up to €2 million but may not exceed a company's equity at the time of the loan's disbursement. The contract fee is up to 1 per cent of the loan amount and the lending period is generally 3-5 years. The rate of interest on a capital loan ranges from 8.5 per cent to 15 per cent, with the part of the interest capitalized or payable in the form of success-based payments at the end of the loan period.

Source: UNECE, based on www.kredex.ee.

Direct financial support

Governments can also target IHGEs via direct financial support (e.g. vouchers, grants or reimbursable loans to support investment in R&D and innovation activities to develop proof of concepts, prototypes and testing). **It is important to ensure that direct financing measures adhere to the principle of additionality and that policies do not crowd out private investors or entrepreneurs while simultaneously targeting clear market failures**.

In the EESC sub-region, several measures have been introduced. The (OECD, 2020) notes that while *"all countries have introduced some form of direct financial support, the design, size and take-up of such instruments vary widely".* For example, the Belarusian Innovation Fund[23] provides innovation vouchers (up to US$25,000) and grants (up to US$100,000) to assist entrepreneurs at each phase of the innovation project, from research and design through to production and commercialization. GITA in Georgia (Figure 2.17) has developed a structured mix of matched advisory and financial support that aims to support start-ups in each development stage, including the growth stage. The Innovation Matching Grants award financing of between €40,000 and €200,000 to develop products, processes or services (or innovative uses of existing ones) that are new at least to the Georgian market and with preference given to projects that enable the provision of services to international markets. These tools have proven popular among target companies, with several hundred applications received by GITA each year (OECD, 2020).

Figure 2.17 • GITA's support pipeline for innovative start-ups – from idea to growth stage

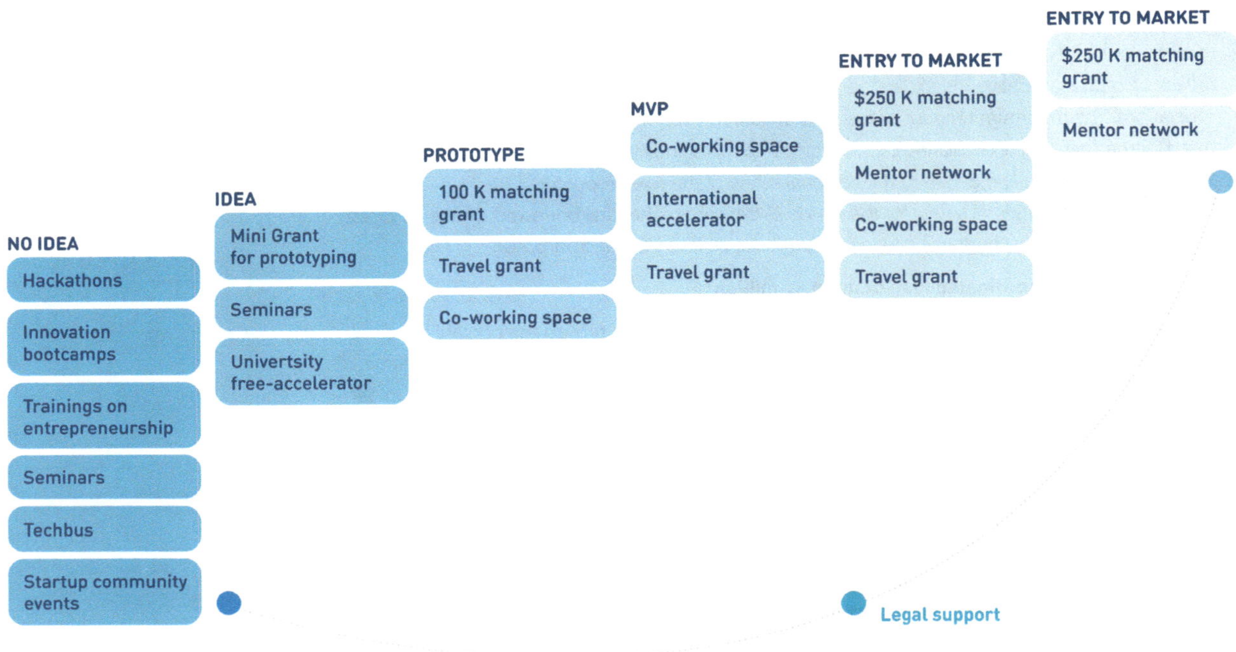

Source: UNECE, adapted from https://gita.gov.ge/

Equity financing

While such grants can be critical in supporting specific stages in the design and development of innovative products and services, **IHGEs generally require access to external equity capital to support their product development, operations and expansion phases into international markets**. Hence, the regulatory environment for investors (crowdfunding, angel investors, private equity funds) to be able to invest and exit in confidence is of critical importance.

The (OECD, 2020) underlines that *"venture capital remains in its infancy across the region, with efforts focusing on building a conducive ecosystem"*. Interviewees stressed that while access to equity capital is an issue, this essentially reflects the lack of suitable regulatory frameworks for investors (investor protection laws) as well as exit paths (initial public offerings, trade sales, etc) in most of the EESC countries, although Armenia and Georgia have advanced further in their efforts to align with international standards[24].

Equity financing is more suited for IHGEs ventures and governments can play a catalysing role in equity market development in the EESC sub-region. For entrepreneurs with an innovation idea, pre-seed and seed funding can help them test their concept (ideation, proof of concept, product design, etc.), while start-up or early-stage funding can then be used to further develop a new company, including during the first commercialization of its products or services.

At the pre-seed/seed/start-up phase, instruments such as equity crowdfunding can be used to attract a pool of small investors with, unfortunately, generally lower investor protection unless crowdfunding has been given a legal framework. At the European level, a new **Regulation on European Crowdfunding Service Providers (ECSP)** for business entered into force in November 2020 which lays down uniform rules across the EU for the provision of investment-based and lending-based crowdfunding services related to business financing. It allows platforms to apply for an EU passport based on a single set of rules, which makes it easier for them to offer their services across the EU with a single authorization. Investors on crowdfunding platforms will benefit from an aligned and enhanced investor protection framework, based on:

- Procedures on information disclosure for projects and crowdfunding platforms;
- Rules on governance and risk management for crowdfunding platforms;
- Strong and harmonized supervisory powers for national authorities overseeing the functioning of crowdfunding platforms.

Some of the EESC countries have recognized the opportunities offered through crowdfunding, with both Georgia and Armenia currently working to introduce regulation and some examples of equity crowdfunding already exist in the region with no governing instruments well developed yet. A key point of interest here is that EU ECSP regulation provides a model legal framework which the EESC countries could use when preparing their respective legislation in this regard.

Equity based crowdfunding initiatives are emerging across Europe, ranging from established players such as **Invesdor Group** (operating two digital investment platforms: Invesdor.com and Finnest.com) (Box 2.12) which has raised almost €30 million worth of investments in Nordic and German companies in 2020 (average investment size was approximately €4,860); to new platforms in countries such as Romania where the recently established **Seedblink**[25] has run 36 campaigns with total investments of €13.1 million of which 55 per cent through crowd-investing (as of March 2021).

Developing an EESC-crowdfunding alliance (as in the Nordic region) could foster a coordinated effort to put in place the necessary regulatory framework and build a large market of investment opportunities and investors across all six countries. This would be beneficial because, as with any investment type, it is important for investors in equity crowdfunding to spread their money across at least 10 investments (the same applies to business angels).

Box 2.12 Equity crowdfunding helps boost development of an innovative Medtech firm

In 2020, the Medtech company **Injeq** raised €2 million with their third equity issue and became the first company to have raised more than €5 million in total via the Invesdor equity crowdfunding platform. Injeq's equity issue was fully subscribed to in under 30 hours on the platform. The company's two previous funding rounds on Invesdor.com, held in 2017 and 2019, raised €1.65 million and €1.69 million respectively. Injeq was founded in 2010 in Tampere (Finland) with a vision of a smart needle that knows where its tip is. The idea is to make lumbar punctures (also knowns as spinal taps) easier: the company hopes to see the smart needle's first applications in the treatment of child leukaemia patients and new-born intensive care wards.

Source: UNECE, based on https ://www.invesdor.com/en-gb/

Business accelerator programmes, also called "start-up factories" (NESTA, 2013) give early-stage and developing companies access to mentorship, investors and other support that help them become stable, self-sufficient businesses. Later stage equity funding can then drive the expansion of a soundly operating company.

An accelerator programme model comprises five main features which set it apart from other approaches to investment or business incubation:

- An application process that is open to all yet highly competitive;
- Provision of pre-seed investment, usually in exchange for equity;
- A focus on small teams rather than individual founders;
- Time-limited support comprising programmed events and intensive mentoring;
- Cohorts or "classes" of start-ups rather than individual companies.

Accelerators are already established across the EESC sub-region, often operating in partnership with accelerators in Western Europe or North America. Interviewees stressed that these partnerships also help start-up with growth potential to go international and, given the legal issues for investors in the sub-region, many of the start-ups supported via the accelerators incorporate in the US or the EU to attract investors (business angels and venture funds). Nevertheless, if ventures scale successfully, they can provide important role models for the local start-up ecosystem and often maintain operations in their home country.

Angel and VC funding

Fostering an investor-friendly ecosystem requires both an appropriate legal framework (e.g. for crowdfunding or private equity) as well as **measures to inform, train and create a network of investors and business angels** (high-worth individuals and experienced former business owners with capital to invest). Few angel investors have the time or financial resources to find and fully fund a portfolio of 10 or more companies themselves. Business angel networks or groups are formed with the goal of sharing deal flow and due diligence work while also pooling funds to make larger investments to secure more favourable terms[26]. Angel networks can also work collectively to raise regulatory and policy issues with governments, undertakings that can contribute to the creation of new and better policies which create the environment for more efficient and effective business growth.

Business angel networks exist in all the EESC countries but the scale of funding from business angels remains limited in most cases. In Armenia, the Science and Technology Angels Network (STAN) brings together a group of prominent Armenian professionals from across the globe to invest in Armenian seed-stage start-ups engaged in science and technology innovation[27]. STAN is hosted by the FAST Foundation which has a set of targets to raise US$620,000 in angel investment. In addition to STAN, the Business Angel Network of Armenia is another network of investors, entrepreneurs and executives from Armenia located domestically and abroad that are interested in making investments in start-up companies[28].

Box 2.13 Examples of accelerator initiatives in the EESC

TechMinsk was founded in 2013 in Belarus with the support of USAID and is based at the Imaguru Start-up HUB. TechMinsk is designed to help top innovative start-ups from the region scale globally and through 10 completed batches, working with 500+ mentors, they have created a cohort of start-ups which are now operating in different countries across the globe and which raised more than US$125 million in investment.

Another accelerator in Belarus is **Bridgio** which has a focus on corporate ventures (spin-offs) notably in the Medtech/Digital Health and industrial and infrastructure IoT.

In Azerbaijan, **Sup VC** was the country's first start-up accelerator having been established in 2015. It works in partnership with other initiatives such as INNOLAND, an incubation, acceleration, co-working and IT education centre. The greatest opportunities for the development of Azerbaijani IHGEs are in the fields such as Agritech, energy and e-commerce, with the first two of these being sectors in which Azerbaijan has traditionally specialized and has a workforce with considerable expertise and talent.

In Armenia, the **ImpactAIM Venture Accelerator**[a] supports start-ups by addressing specific challenges related to the sustainable development goals. The ImpactAim Accelerator brings together the private sector and development agencies to exit solutions and start-ups that are targeting the development of a specific sector (for example Agriculture, Climate, Education or Food Production) and have sustainable business models that can be further scaled.

In Georgia, GITA has partnered with the global 500 Start-ups platform to launch the **500Georgia acceleration programme**[b] which includes a combination of intensive and remote training over the course of seven months. At the end of this period, staff from a selected group of companies will be invited to spend 4 weeks in San Francisco for an immersion experience focused on developing their global mindset and helping prepare for international expansion.

In Moldova, **TEKWILL** and the **XY Accelerator** have launched a programme, with the support of USAID and SIDA, to encourage young people to grow their businesses from scratch and become competitive in large markets. In 2020, the XY Accelerator team delivered 1,280 hours of mentoring over four months to five start-ups. The TEKWILL project supported the delivery of mentoring and consulting under the accelerator, and financial support was provided by local investors to two start-ups.

In Ukraine, three accelerator organisations are located in the **Unit.City** innovation park, including a platform for scaling manufacturing projects called INDAX and Radar Tech which develops and launches corporate accelerators. Additionally, Unit.City also contains the Sector X Accelerator which provides a range of programmes aimed at either helping start-ups access their first clients in the US or promote the development of Femtech, Deeptech and Greentech projects.

Source: Author's analysis for UNECE.
[a] https://impactaim.com/
[b] https://ecosystems.500.co/500georgia

Box 2.14 Open innovation and crowdsourcing – Innovation DTEK in Ukraine

An interesting open innovation approach that is close to a model of corporate venturing is the **Innovation DTEK crowdsourcing platform** in Ukraine that seeks to attract innovative solutions to challenges in the energy sector.

DTEK Group is the leader in Ukraine's energy sector and the industry's biggest private investor. It recently launched the Innovation DTEK platform where DTEK publishes queries to find teams, ideas and technologies to address topical issues. With the help of this platform, DTEK seeks to collect innovative ideas aimed particularly at increasing the level of safety, business efficiency and environmental friendliness of its production. DTEK uses an innovation crowdsourcing method to develop solutions, recognising that that technical progress cannot only rely on internal resources.

Source: UNECE, based on https://openinnovation.dtek.com/en.

In Belarus, the Angels Band network[29] has more than 90 investors, many of which have been trained in the Business Angels Academy. Angles Band is a partner of the High-Tech Park and they maintain partnerships with other Belarusian start-up ecosystem players such as RBF Ventures, Bulba Ventures, Haxus Ventures, and the Imaguru Start-up Hub.

UAngel[30] is a Ukrainian business angel network providing a platform for entrepreneurs to meet investors and for investors to locally and internationally syndicate. It is a closed group of high net-worth individuals or entities interested in financing start-ups in their early stage of development. A business angels' network that gathers experienced businesspeople and top managers for investment in start-up companies also exists in Moldova[31].

Box 2.15 Building an investor ecosystem – services for investors in the Nordic and Baltic area

While the Nordic countries (Denmark, Estonia, Finland, Latvia, Lithuania, Norway and Sweden) are more developed in terms of their financial investment systems than the EESC countries, the seven Nordic national markets remain limited in scale and potential deal-flow for investors. Structured co-operation through the NordicBAN network enables both access for start-ups to a broader pool of investors and the provision of services and training to angels interested in cross-border investing.

NordicBAN represents 12 Nordic and Baltic angel networks which cover over 2200 business angels. Their main activities include mapping the new Nordic area (Nordic and Baltic) angel activity and providing the start-up ecosystem with best practice when it comes to angel investment.

The focus of the services is to support angels to link-up with each other and entrepreneurs and to offer tools to support cross-border investments by offering:

- Access to +200 Nordic Angels - filtered according to industry and region;
- Syndication ready start-ups with an active lead investor already onboard;
- Tools and templates – such as investment contracts and various cross-border materials.

Source: UNECE, based on https://www.nordicban.net.

Despite the existing networks in the EESC sub-region, business angel investment potential is still nascent and more needs to be done to develop the expertise (e.g. dedicated training programmes for investors) needed for seed and early-stage investment. The European Business Angel Network (EBAN)[32] report for 2019 only provides data for two EESC countries: one network in Ukraine with 50 investors and 21 investments with a total value of €6.1 million (essentially into IT hardware and online services) and one network in Belarus with 82 investors which made 3 investments for a total of €1.1 million. Various examples of national and cross-border co-operation in building investor ecosystems (including practical tools for investors, templates for contracting, etc.) exist around the world and can be used to inspire and inform the development of investor (business angel) ecosystems in the EESC sub-region (see Box 2.15).

A business angel investment is normally a minority investment (usually 10-30 per cent), and it is directed at the pre-seed, seed or early stage and start-up phase. Moreover, angels increasingly invest in syndicates (groups) and alongside seed VC funds. In the EU, the average business angel investment is approximately €25,000 while the average investment (total for syndicated or group of investors) per company is about €180,000. The individual angel and average total investment per company in the EESC sub-region is likely to be lower. Interviewees noted that **beyond an investment range of €100,000 it is generally difficult to secure equity or other forms of non-bank finance from national sources in the EESC sub-region.**

Venture capitalists primarily make later stage minority investments (venture investments) or expansion majority investments (buy-outs). As the (OECD, 2020) notes, VC is on the whole still in its infancy in the six EESC countries…*"as the establishment and success of VCs is heavily dependent on growth potential of enterprises, the investment readiness of companies and a policy framework that allows for equity investment, all of which is hampered in the EESC region".* Critically, **none of the countries has progressed significantly in developing dedicated legal frameworks to facilitate VC investments**, which along with the absence of obvious "local" exit routes (IPOs, institutional investors, etc.), limit investors' appetite and opportunities. As interviewees noted, given the current legal framework and lack of sophistication of the investor ecosystem, **the typical start-up route in the EESC sub-region for innovative companies with growth potential is to incorporate in the US (Delaware) or certain EU locations (such as Estonia via the e-residency formula)**.

The most advanced countries (see Box 2.16) in terms of VC in the EESC sub-region are Armenia, Belarus and Ukraine (the latter, due to its size, offers a potentially greater deal flow) as equity finance is somewhat more developed and there is now some accumulated and relevant experience with equity investment in IHGEs that can provide inspiration for other the countries in the region (see Annex for the two Armenian examples).

A framework for effective investment ecosystems

To further develop the investment ecosystem for IHGEs, policymakers can take a number of steps (Table 2.10) to boost supply (more investors), improve demand (enhance the quality and the number of firms looking for investment) and optimize market impacts (through encouraging and supporting syndication and networking of investors, etc.).

Box 2.16 Equity and venture capital initiatives in the EESC

Zubr Capital[a] is the first private equity firm based in Belarus. Their major focus is on **innovative and high-tech companies** and they have primarily invested in companies driving the digital transformation, e-commerce, printing and educational tech. They are interested in the development of early-stage investment and they participate in the Angels Band network.

In 2016, Zubr Capital launched the US$50 million Zubr Capital Fund I (ZCFI) with the European Bank for Reconstruction and Development (EBRD) as an anchor investor. Another major investor of the ZCFI was WGVC Limited, an investment organization managed by the founders of Wargaming. A second closure of the ZCFI fund took place in January 2018 and almost doubled the fund size to more than US$90 million. The fund anchor investor remains the EBRD, which increased its investment in ZCFI with another major investor, the Dutch Development Fund, which invested US$15 million. The aim of the Dutch Development Fund investment is to support the development of the private equity industry in the region and the introduction of environmental and social management systems in Belarusian companies. The ZCFI aims to invest in 10-12 fast-growing Belarusian companies and thus far has invested in nine firms.

One ZCFI investment has been in MediaCube[b], a company which was launched in 2016 and has grown to have a "global footprint" as an official partner of YouTube as well as TikTok and one of the top 25 video content copyright holders in the world. Mediacube is engaged in the monetization of video and music content, the development of its own IT solutions for creators and musicians as well as distribution and copyright protection. Clients of MediaCube are YouTube-content creators along with well-known brands and artists from 64 countries. The company has now grown to have more than 150 employees.

Granatus Ventures[c], founded in 2013, is the first VC firm with offices in Yerevan, London and Singapore providing investment, networks and expertize to start-ups worldwide that **leverage Armenia's potential as an emerging technology hub**. Granatus Ventures has made investments in fields ranging from AI software development such as Krisp and IntelAir for crop monitoring for farmers to food delivery. Granatus Ventures manages a portfolio of 14 high-tech start-ups that have cumulatively attracted more than **US$62 million** in capital from leading VCs in Silicon Valley and Europe.

According to Granatus Ventures co-founder and managing partner, the start-up ecosystem in Armenia offers dynamic prospects with new and exciting opportunities in **deep tech** and companies that apply **scientific knowledge and discoveries for commercial opportunities**. For example, in 2020, Granatus Ventures and cLAB Ventures entered into a general partnership agreement to find and invest in cancer diagnostics and treatment start-ups that develop life-saving innovations. Moreover, in 2019, the UNDP signed an agreement with Granatus Ventures to establish and manage the Tech4SDG Fund. This fund, with a target size of US$40 million, will make investments in technology-driven ventures globally that demonstrate strong potential for social and environmental impacts.

Also in **Armenia**, in 2019 the EU and the EBRD agreed to provide up to €16 million to support the launch of the **Amber Capital EU-Armenia SME Fund**[d]. This new private equity fund seeks to raise a total of **€70 million** to invest in SMEs in Armenia. The fund will be managed by an international investment firm with an office and team of professionals established in Armenia and will seek to build a diversified investment portfolio across various sectors including renewable energy, agriculture, manufacturing, tourism, information technology and logistics.

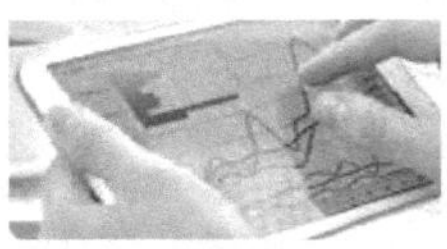

The **Ukrainian Venture Capital and Private Equity Association (UVCA)** was established in mid-2014 following the example of the European Venture Capital and Private Equity Association (InvestEurope[e]) and currently lays claim to 50 members comprised of private equity and venture funds, accelerators, incubators,

educational institutions, and non-government organizations that have a significant impact on the development of the Ukrainian investment market. The association promotes investment opportunities in Ukraine for foreign investment funds, conducts market research, lobbies the Government to improve the investment and business climate and carries out activities on behalf of Invest in Ukraine.

Box 2.16 Equity and venture capital initiatives in the EESC (Concluded)

In 2019, the UVCA[f] recorded **111 VC investments worth US$509.9 million**, a 50 per cent increase on 2018, with most investment into the growth stage of various businesses (US$439 million). The average deal size was US$5.7 million but the average "ticket" at growth stage was US$110 million and the top 5 deals accounted for 87 per cent of VC investment in Ukraine in 2019. The largest deal was done by GitLab, a system for managing a program code repository, with US$268 million raised at the growth stage. Most VC investment was into **software** (US$272 million) with **online services and hardware** being the second most invested in sector and where the origin of the capital was largely the USA. There were also 29 exits in 2019, up from 8 in 2018.

The UVCA 2019 report also identifies six deals in companies with substantive R&D (based on R&D staff employed in Ukraine) underlining the potential for **tech-based development**, building on the success of companies such as **Grammarly and GitLab** which qualify as unicorns.

Source: Author's analysis for UNECE.
[a] https://zubrcapital.com/
[b] https://mediacube.co/about
[c] https://www.granatusventures.com/
[d] https://www.ebrd.com/news/2019/ebrd-and-european-union-support-launch-of-private-equity-fund-in-armenia.html
[e] https://www.investeurope.eu/
[f] http://uvca.eu/en/news/investments-into-ukrainian-startups-in-2019-overview

Public sector intervention in the equity market is made via three main mechanisms:

- *The "equity carry" model (portage)* – a contractual arrangement where a Government acquires equity shares from private investors for a fixed period and sells them back at a pre-specified price in the future.
- *A "co-investment" model with two types of governmental support: i) a privately managed government-backed venture capital (VC) fund that invests on a non-exclusive basis in innovative companies; and ii) public investment as a co-limited partner in a privately managed venture capital fund.*
- *The "fund-of-funds" model* requiring the establishment of a public fund that takes minority equity stakes in existing or new privately-managed VC funds.

Table 2.10 What policymakers can do to foster business angel investments

Supply - generating more investors	Demand - quality deal flow	Market Impact and sustainability
Investment friendly tax environment	Investment readiness (incl. regional training and support)	Support for sustainable and professional BANs
Co-investment funds	Financial literacy at schools	Data collection
Investor readiness training sessions	Entrepreneurial mind-set development (incl. links with local businesses)	Local BA/VC forums
Media campaigns	Incubators and other facilitators to educate and prepare entrepreneurs	Light regulation for early-stage investment market

Source: UNECE, based on (European Commission, 2015).

In terms of legal and operational complexity, the **equity carry model is the simplest and has proven useful in countries with underdeveloped capital markets**. However, it tends to have limited spill-over effects in promoting the development of a domestic VC sector and enhancing competition among potential VC investors. The other two models, involving co-investment and a fund-of-funds, require the presence of already established innovation infrastructure, including active business angels and VC investors, in addition to a more advanced legal and operational environment. They also require a high level of confidence by private VC investors in a country's legal system, rule of law conditions as well as tax and public policy transparency.

These models have proven effective in, *inter alia*, the EU, the US and Israel in the early stages of the development of an investor ecosystem and VC market. Experience suggests that co-investment funds and fund-of-funds, both of which seek to leverage private sector investment, are likely be more effective than direct public equity funds.

Co-investment funds have also proven to be an effective instrument, limiting the risks associated with market distortions due to government intervention as public investment only occurs when it is at least matched by private equity investments from business angels or venture capitalists. For example, the European Investment Fund (EIF) has partnered with a range of national investment bodies to establish co-investment vehicles (see the figure below).

The **fund-of-funds mechanism** has also been extensively utilized across Europe to ensure public investment is used effectively to leverage private funds. Examples include multi-country level initiatives in the Baltic States and the Western Balkans specifically targeting investments in innovative companies.

- *The EIF and Bank Gospodarstwa Krajowego (BGK) Fund of Funds* stimulates equity investment into growth-focussed enterprises in Poland and the CEE region. At first closing, this fund-of-funds had a commitment of €90 million with a target size of €180 million at final closing[33].
- *Baltic Innovation Fund 2 (BIF 2)*[34] is a €156 million fund-of-funds initiative launched by the EIF in co-operation with the Baltic national investment agencies KredEx (Estonia), Altum (Latvia) and Invega (Lithuania). It builds on the success of BIF 1, its predecessor programme. BIF 2 will manage investments into private equity and venture capital funds focused on the Baltic States over a period of 5 years (from July 2019) to boost equity investments into SMEs with high-growth potential.

- *The Enterprise Innovation Fund (ENIF)*[35] is focused on tech companies in the Balkans. The €40 million fund is dedicated primarily to early-stage and growth investments. Within the fund's "seed pocket", €1.5 million is allocated for investments of up to €100,000 per company. The majority of the fund is allocated for early stage and growth investments of up to €3 million per company. These investments are intended to fuel the international business expansion and growth of the most promising tech start-ups that can show traction and prove their potential to "make it big".

Figure 2.18 • Example of a co-investment fund programme (the Netherlands)

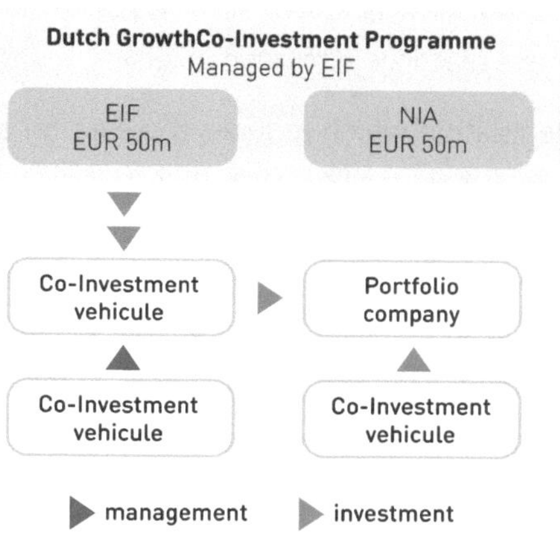

- The Dutch Growth Co-Investment Programme is managed by EIF, and funded by Netherlands Investment Agency (NIA) and EIF
- The Dutch Growth Co-Investment Programme provides co-investment funding to qualified fund managers with an established relationship with EIF
- Eligibility is determined by EIF, based on criteria on the target company and purpose of financing
- The funding is provided through a co-investment vehicle, set up an managed by the fund manager
- The fund manager invests in the company from the co-investment vehicle alongside the main investment fund, in which EIF is an investor

Source: UNECE, adapted from https://www.eif.org/what_we_do/resources/dutch-growth-co-investment-programme/index.htm

A similar multi-country fund-of-funds to support the development of the investment ecosystem across the six EESC countries could be examined. In the Western Balkans, the ENIF is part of the Western Balkans Enterprise Development & Innovation Facility (WB EDIF), a joint initiative of the EU, International Financial Institutions (including the EIB, EIF, EBRD, and the World Bank), bilateral partners (Italian, Austrian, etc.) and the public institutions of the Western Balkans economies (Figure 2.19).

Figure 2.19 • WB EDIF package of funding and support services

Source: UNECE, adapted from http://www.wbedif.eu/about-wbedif/

Via this structure, WB EDIF leverages upon the expertise of 27 international, regional and local market players providing not only equity funding but also regarding loan guarantees and support services to providers and policymakers. Such a model would provide the EESC countries with expertize, long-term financing and associated technical assistance.

2.2.4 Reinforcing firms' in-house capabilities to grow: skills and talent

Access to educated and skilled staff is essential for any viable business. However, **for IHGEs the range and type of expertise needed is likely to be significantly more demanding to source** (including advanced technological know-how, language skills and understanding of international market trends as well as business practices in target markets).

Overly stringent employment protection legislation which reduces the ease for skilled employees to shift between firms leads to less dynamic firm growth, especially in R&D intensive sectors, which in turn leads to significantly lower productivity growth (OECD, 2020). The ease of finding skilled employees ranges from 4.8 out of 7 in Azerbaijan to 3.2 in Moldova (WEF, 2019) suggesting that in all EESC countries there is room for improving the skills base. In addition, World Bank Enterprise Survey data confirms that an inadequately educated workforce is a significantly more frequent obstacle than employment (labour) regulations. An EU survey of IHGEs (European Commission, 2015) along with[36] (Vlerick Business School, 2020), based on an analysis of European scale-ups, found that **finding and retaining high-quality employees is the biggest challenge for fast-growing companies in the EU (30 per cent of scale-ups)**.

For IHGEs, the challenge is to **source graduates in science, technology, engineering and mathematics who also have the needed know-how gained through a complementary entrepreneurial and financial education**. The six EESC countries have relatively high levels of tertiary graduates in STEM[37] which undeniably constitutes an advantage in this regard, however, the **entrepreneurial, business and financial management skills** required to create or develop an IHGE need further development. Given the uncertain nature of many high-growth ventures, entrepreneurial, business and financial management skills are critical for IHGE success as they comprise a range of traits that are both cognitive (e.g. opportunity spotting, risk assessment) and behavioural (teamwork, mobilizing resources) (OECD, 2020). All the EESC countries have a defined policy commitment to entrepreneurial learning but there is varying progress in implementing entrepreneurial learning in both education and SME policies.

Three main types of policy support are commonly used to make sure the necessary skillsets as well as creative and specialized staff are available to potential IHGEs (and more broadly to SMEs in general):

- Entrepreneurial education focused on specific skillsets necessary to develop IHGEs;
- Ensuring access for IHGEs to STEM graduates as well as other specialized skills (including design, marketing and international business know-how); and
- Talent attraction (start-up and IT visas, etc.) as well as measures to avoid 'brain-drain' from the sub-region's economies.

Leadership skills for IHGEs

Taking a longer-term perspective, the **importance of incorporating entrepreneurial education into the educational curricula from the primary school level upwards is now widely acknowledged as a game changer**.

> *"A growth mindset has specific features that set it apart from a more "generic" entrepreneurial mindset. Entrepreneurship curricula should therefore not just try to encourage students to consider entrepreneurship as a career option but equip them with the* ***mindsets of growth entrepreneurs.*** *This may involve changing the content, format and learning environments of entrepreneurial education, and the actors that shape these. This ideally should cover the full education spectrum, from primary school to university"* (NESTA, 2019).

Curricula for entrepreneurial skills adjusted to growth companies should:

- *Incorporate real-life role models from the region* (drawn from the EESC sub-region, wider central and Eastern Europe as well as the Baltic countries) rather than only using case material that explains how IHGEs developed in more advanced or larger economies (US, Western Europe, Asia). Interviewees stressed the importance of promoting role models and learning from their experience to inspire other innovative entrepreneurs to aim for growth.
- *Focus not only on the skills* needed to have an entrepreneurial mind-set or to launch a 'start-up' *but also the process of growth and scaling companies* via the skills (in-house) and networks (peers, investors, etc.) required at each growth stage.

Research also showed that innovative companies in their growth stage perform better when backed by equity investors (Vlerick Business School, 2020), which highlights the importance of educating and training potential IHGE managers to be open-minded enough and equipped to work with external investors (notably business angels that bring both capital and experience). There is a range of leadership programmes that emphasize the skills required for high growth delivered by business schools, enterprise agencies and private training providers. These, along with the UK ScaleUp searchable directory of support programmes can provide inspiration for the EESC countries to develop tailored programmes for managers of potential IHGEs (Box 2.17).

In most of the EESC sub-region, business leadership training programmes are already being offered, hence, there is no need to start from scratch but rather to learn from and partner with some of the top international leadership for growth programme providers.

Ensuring IHGEs have access to skilled employees

Interviewees in the EESC sub-region highlighted the need to evolve education and training aimed at filling specific skills gaps, notably those related to IT skills, including coding and machine learning. Moreover, **long-term improvements and increased investment in STEM and entrepreneurial education in national education systems were viewed as potentially more important than specific short-term initiatives to fill gaps**. The OECD's SME Policy Index (OECD, 2020) notes that "disruptive technological change is opening up new growth prospects which skills gaps and mismatches risk damaging.

Box 2.17 Examples of management training programmes for growth-oriented businesses: Ireland and Scotland

Enterprise Ireland's Leadership 4 Growth initiative was established in 2006 to build on the leadership talent within Irish indigenous industry and ultimately seeks to increase job and wealth creation in Ireland. Over the following 14 years the programme has transformed how CEOs lead themselves, their companies and their people, to international success.

Enterprise Ireland has partnered with the best educators in the world to deliver Leadership 4 Growth, with **400 CEOs** having taken part to date. An evaluation, carried out in 2015, found that the participants exceeded the export growth of a control group of companies by on average 55 per cent and improved their sales per employee ratio by 15 per cent more than the control group on average each year following their programme participation.

The programme is designed to build and enhance the strategic leadership capabilities of ambitious CEOs and managing directors. The Leadership 4 Growth programme aims to equip business leaders with the necessary visionary, strategic and innovative capabilities required to scale sustainable companies on the global stage. It is delivered in partnership with the IESE Business School and the Learning Partnership. Leadership 4 Growth supports CEO's to:

- *Identify their own personal leadership potential* and capability through the development of their leadership style, ambition and confidence;
- *Strategically analyse and evaluate* their own business to make strategic choices for rapid growth;
- *Create a Strategic Growth Action Plan* and robust strategic management/deployment framework for rapid growth and sustainability;
- *Identify and develop their personal leadership* with the C-Suite[b] and the board to grow a strong effective team to execute and implement step changes arising from the growth plan;
- *Understand the behaviour* required to operate a culture of coaching/learning for continuous transformation and employee engagement.

The programme comprises three overseas week-long residential modules which cover dynamic business strategy, high-performance leadership and sustainable growth. Each module is followed by a one-day Ireland-based Insights Session involving the participant's senior leadership team. Throughout the programme, each participant is assigned a business adviser to encourage, challenge and assist in implementing their strategic frameworks and apply core leadership concepts to their companies. Customized one-day masterclasses for chief financial officers and chief human resources officers are another additional element to the programme.

Source: UNECE, based on https://www.enterprise-ireland.com/en/funding-supports/Company/Esetablish-SME-Funding/Leadership-4-Growth-Programme.html

Employers already generally lack sufficient high-quality skills, particularly for growing enterprises and export-oriented companies".

In Armenia, Belarus, Georgia and Moldova, training is available for SME staff to increase their digital skills. However, there is still ample room for increased investment in skills intelligence and anticipation of future needs. The TUMO Convergence Centre for Engineering and Applied Science in Yerevan is an example of a focused initiative to build a pool of skills STEM experts, while Unit.City`s UCode IT-Academy in Ukraine is another (Annexes).

Box 2.17 Examples of management training programmes for growth-oriented businesses: Ireland and Scotland (Concluded)

First launched in 2015 the **Growth Advantage Programme (GAP)**[c] **at Strathclyde University** provides relevant, accessible and practical learning for fast-growing Scottish businesses embarking on the scale-up journey.

It is aimed at existing businesses with a minimum GBP 1 million turnover with real growth ambitions and recommended participants are the founding managing director, chief executive or principal of the business with a significant ownership interest. Businesses come from all over Scotland, from a wide range of sectors and include companies started from scratch, bought and multi-generation family businesses – all with ambitions to grow.

Independent evaluators found that the average annual turnover of programme participants is 15.9 percentage points higher than that of a control group, while the average growth in employee numbers is 10.9 percentage points higher. Furthermore, the first cohort of participants saw turnover growth of 17.6 per cent one year after starting the programme and cumulative turnover growth after four years rose to 67 per cent.

Participants are offered a **programme that links high-quality executive education with the insights and shared learning that comes from peer networks.** Business leaders attend an initial one-day orientation meeting and four two-day workshops that take place over 10 months. GAP's focus is on the practical application of research for growing businesses as well as on peer learning. Each workshop concludes with the creation of a 60-day action plan which is reviewed at the start of the next workshop.

Strathclyde University also provides practical support with GAP cohorts having access to project support from the Hunter Centre of Entrepreneurship, product design resources from the Engineering Faculty and access to talent through the University Careers Service.

Source: Author's analysis for UNECE.
[a] https://www.enterprise-ireland.com/en/funding-supports/Company/Esetablish-SME-Funding/Leadership-4-Growth-Programme.html
[b] C-suite refers to the executive-level managers within a company. Common c-suite executives include chief executive officer (CEO), chief financial officer (CFO), chief operating officer (COO), and chief information officer (CIO)
[c] See: https://www.strath.ac.uk/business/huntercentreforentrepreneurship/gap/

When it comes to accessing talent for operating companies, the recruitment of staff can be facilitated by using new technologies such as AI to support the process of reaching out to and hiring skilled staff[38]. Moreover, Hackathons and other industry or tech specific events can be used to identify promising (software) engineers, etc. For example, in Armenia, the Catalyst Foundation[39] runs initiatives to feed the Armenian start-up ecosystem with the relevant skillset and a pipeline of capable companies such as the **Armenia Start-up Academy, Hero House**, an AI Incubator or the entrepreneurial assistant school, etc. However, the skills required by potential IHGEs in the future are not only technological as the survey results for Armenia[40] indicate that there is an **increasing demand for soft skills** such as innovative and creative thinking, active learning, originality, leadership and social influence, critical thinking, and problem-solving skills.

Mechanisms for mapping and identifying skills gaps and fostering rapid upskilling and retraining should be part of the policy toolkit for IHGEs in the EESC sub-region.

Talent retention and attraction

Many countries have sought to make it easier for those looking to start a firm with high potential to locate and establish business in their country. Finland[41], Estonia[42] and Lithuania[43], for example, have done so by **making start-up permits or visas available**. Such visas can be attractive parts of an overall package offered by countries or cities positioning themselves as "entrepreneurial or tech hubs". **However, and most importantly, they should be part of a credible, broader policy package aimed at developing an entrepreneurial high-growth ecosystem.** Visas or e-residency type measures (see Box 2.18) alone will be unlikely to attract entrepreneurs to set up their businesses in a country.

Campaigns promoting entrepreneurial ecosystems of the six EESC countries as places for entrepreneurs to develop and grow IHGES and as attractive locations to live and work for skilled people should be a core element of any such policy toolkit.

Box 2.18 Azerbaijan e- and m-Residency programme

Azerbaijan has made efforts to become more attractive to global entrepreneurs, launching in 2017 the Digital Trade Hub (DTH) to help develop the digital ecosystem and attract foreign investors and small business owners. One of the DTH's major initiatives so far has been the introduction of the electronic residency (e-Residency) and mobile residency (m-Residency) programme in 2018, a move that made Azerbaijan the second country in the world (after Estonia) to offer an e-Residency programme aimed at the provision of easy, fast and reliable services to foreign investors and businesses, and the first country in the world to offer m-Residency.

The m-Residency programme provides virtual government-verified identification in Azerbaijan and successful applicants receive a specially issued Asan Imza (Mobile ID) SIM card for secure authentication and electronic signatures. With this, it is possible to start official activities in the country and use any banking service. Although international applications currently come with limitations, the m-Residency programme has high-growth ambitions.

Source: UNECE, based on https://dth.az/index

Countries that face deficits in specific skillsets set have developed sophisticated campaigns to attract and facilitate the location of people with specific expertise or knowledge in certain key business sectors. **Business Finland's #FinlandWorks campaign** mixes social media (e.g. a dedicated page on LinkedIn) with a website that provides support to both employers and those looking for work[44]. They also run a Talent Boost programme[45] for companies operating in Finland which aims to bring companies together with the top talents in various fields. The programme also helps companies to internationalize by supporting the recruitment of top international talent.

In **Estonia**, it has become easier for tech companies and start-ups to hire foreign specialists. In 2016, immigration quotas for non-EU specialists who come to Estonia to work for a start-up or a tech company were lifted[46]. This policy has helped tech companies and start-ups to hire hundreds of non-EU employees. According to Start-up Estonia, 18 per cent of the employees in Estonia's start-up sector are foreigners and companies are keen to bring more outside talent into Estonia[47]. More recently, Estonia has also launched a new **Digital Nomad Visa**[48] that allows remote workers to live in Estonia and legally work for their employer or their own company registered abroad[49]. As of August 2020, eligible location-independent workers can apply for the chance to come to Estonia to live for up to a year knowing that they can legally work.

2.2.5 Going global: networking and scaling in international markets

The six EESC countries have differing arrangements in terms of trade bloc memberships and market access, especially in the relationships with the neighbouring EU and Eurasian Economic Union (EAEU) blocs. Three countries, Georgia, Moldova and Ukraine, all have access to the European Single Market[50] in selected sectors and grant EU investors in those sectors a regulatory environment that is aligned as far as possible to that in the EU[51]. Armenia and Belarus are part of the Russian Federation-led EAEU [52]. Moreover, all EESC countries, except for Belarus and Azerbaijan, are WTO members[53]. **These differing trade arrangements influence the potential of IHGEs in the six countries to attract investors and enter foreign markets**, although this depends on the type of product or service offered. IHGEs from the EESC sub-region providing digital services (e-commerce, software, etc.) are likely to find it easier to sell to consumers or other businesses than, for example, IHGEs exporting more heavily regulated products such as financial services or medical equipment.

Internationalization strategies for businesses are a part of state action implemented, *inter alia*, through export promotion agencies. Nevertheless, these agencies are often under-developed in terms of the range and sophistication of support they provide. Besides government missions, other organizations and donors implement different programmes to promote internationalization and access to foreign markets. However, according to interviewees, these are not adjusted to the specific needs of IHGEs. **Timely mobilization of expertise on intellectual property and advanced technologies, access to investors in major hubs such as London or the 'Silicon Valley', co-operation partners and insights on global markets are critical to sustaining growth**. As Sten Tamkivi, chief prod*uct officer at talent mobility start-up Topia and previously the general manager at Skype (2005-2013) has noted:*

"You cannot build a billion-dollar company focusing on a market of 1.3 million people. That creates this vibe where everything that you start here starts at least with a European, if not global, mindset."[54]

Many of the elements of the policy toolkit already presented automatically incorporate an international dimension given the necessity to rapidly move from national markets to regional, European or global depending on the business model. Accelerator programmes, finance, leadership training, skills initiatives all build on international expertise to succeed.

A key role in linking potential IHGEs to international markets is often played by investors. (Vlerick Business School, 2020) noted that **external equity investors serve as a catalyst to scale-up internationalization** and their investee companies are therefore more likely to face the difficulties inherent to successfully breaking into new markets. This explains why external equity-funded scale-ups highlight access to international markets as their most important challenge in the Vlerick survey. **Initiatives to bring international equity investors experienced in scaling firms to the EESC sub-region can drive international connections**.

IHGEs may enhance their sales growth by developing a dedicated sales team, a market access strategy and by considering non-organic growth modes (such as acquisitions, joint ventures, or alliances) as well as being foremostly more internationally oriented. International markets may be entered through direct exports but other internationalization modes may be relevant as well. Tailored support provided through account management by enterprise agencies can ensure that companies are given the support they need at the right point in their growth trajectory.

In addition, interviewees stressed **the importance for IHGEs in the EESC sub-region to have access to international networks, whether via government channels** (embassy economic counsellors, etc.) **or, more importantly, via business, education, investor and private (diaspora) networks**. At the current time, the networks in EESC countries are informal, although in most, entrepreneurial foundations, accelerators and investment advisors work to link entrepreneurs with international know-how.

A recent example of the above is the **Armenia Virtual Bridge**[55], which aims to facilitate market launches and business growth for Armenian start-ups via educational programmes and mentoring. The programme, launched by the Ministry of High-Tech Industry in partnership with the Armenian Chamber of Commerce in Silicon Valley, is designed to equip entrepreneurs with the technical, business development and soft skills necessary to grow the company abroad. Interaction with domain experts and time spent in Silicon Valley is expected to enable the entrepreneurs to tap into the diaspora's extensive network for strategic introductions and to help fundraising efforts. The aim was to recruit start-ups that have either created a prototype or have released a product or service (at least in one market, such as Armenia) and now want to launch or grow in international markets. The programme consists of incubation and acceleration components, with the incubation component implemented jointly with Draper University, one of the leading entrepreneurship training programmes in Silicon Valley and where 15 entrepreneurs will be awarded state scholarships to study. Returning to Armenia, it is expected that the acquired knowledge, experience and culture will be transferred to the technology centres and start-ups in the country. The acceleration component of the programme includes the direct participation of the leading Silicon Valley experts, including founders, directors, heads of investment companies, and educators from renowned universities.

Tools used by Western European enterprises agencies to support such linkages include networks such as the **Global Scots network**[56] managed by **Scottish Enterprise**. It is a worldwide network of business contacts (usually of Scottish descent or with a link to Scotland) who are experts in their field and are motivated to help Scottish companies develop, expand and thrive in a competitive international market.

Another example is the creation of five **Nordic Innovation Houses** in important business and tech hubs across the globe by Nordic enterprise agencies. The aim of the initiative is to pool resources of the five Nordic countries to create a common hub providing services and access to a network of contacts in each of the regions (Box 2.19).

To build on such examples, there is a **need to structure relationships with the diaspora networks of the six EESC countries in order to help provide tailored support and access for potential IHGEs to major European and global business networks and locations.**

Box 2.19 Nordic Innovation Houses - supporting international growth

The Nordic Innovation House initiative[a], co-funded by Nordic Innovation and the various Nordic national government enterprise agencies, was launched in September 2014 with the first Nordic Innovation House opening in Silicon Valley. The houses provide a co-working space, incubator and resource centre for Nordic tech companies in global tech hubs.

Based on the positive results of the first house, the network expanded to five Nordic Innovation Houses: the original in Silicon Valley with another four located in New York, Singapore, Hong Kong and Tokyo.

The initiative has developed a Nordic community and network for connecting start-ups to high-quality mentors, networks of investors, business services and funding opportunities in each location.

Source: UNECE, based on https://www.nordicinnovationhouse.com/

[a] See: https://www.nordicinnovationhouse.com/

Notes

1 Presentation by Leah Pape, Scottish Enterprise, UNECE training on IHGEs in EESC, Session 2 at https://unece.org/eci/documents/2021/03/presentations/practitioner-insight-scottish-scale-ecosystem-ensuring-high

2 See: https://www.doingbusiness.org/

3 See https://ec.europa.eu/info/law/law-making-process/planning-and-proposing-law/better-regulation-why-and-how/better-regulation-guidelines-and-toolbox/better-regulation-toolbox_en

4 See for example: https://www.bmwi.de/Redaktion/EN/Dossier/regulatory-test-beds-testing-environments-for-innovation-and-regulation.html or https://www.ofgem.gov.uk/publications-and-updates/energy-regulation-sandbox-guidance-innovators

5 See: https://www.nbg.gov.ge/index.php?m=742

6 See: https://www.moh.gov.sg/home/our-healthcare-system/licensing-experimentation-and-adaptation-programme-(leap)---a-moh-regulatory-sandbox

7 The so-called patent box incentive has also been applied in certain countries to provide lower effective tax rates on income derived from IP. However, its impact on incentivizing innovative local firms to invest in R&D and IP is not proven (Barrios et al, 2015).

8 See: https://moldovaitpark.md

9 https://unece.org/eci/documents/2020/12/working-documents/innovation-sustainable-development-review-georgia-advance-0

10 The dedicated paper to be presented at the UNECE Committee on Innovation Competitiveness and Public-Private Partnerships to take place on 02-04 June 2021.

11 See: https://innovation-procurement.org/

12 See: https://www.civtechalliance.org

13 On this, please see the UNECE policy handbook "Business Incubators for Sustainable Development in the SPECA subregion", forthcoming.

14 Daniel Isenberg and the Babson Entrepreneurship Ecosystem Platform https://hbr.org/2012/11/focus-entrepreneurship-policy work has been used by other countries to prioritise scale-ups.

15 https://www.scaleupinstitute.org.uk

16 https://scale-updenmark.com

17 https://startupeuropeclub.eu/our-projects/

18 https://scaleup4.eu/about/

19 The practice of funding a project or venture by raising money from a large number of people who each contribute a relatively small amount, typically via an internet platform. See also: https://ec.europa.eu/growth/tools-databases/crowdfunding-guide/what-is/explained_en

20 Business angels are conventionally defined as high-net worth individuals who invest their own money, along with their time and expertise, directly in unquoted companies in which they have no family connection in the hope of having financial gain (Mason, 2013).

21 The 2018 OECD enterprise survey of Azerbaijan found that 58 per cent of surveyed SMEs considered insufficient access to finance a barrier to their growth.

22 https://www.isc.am/

23 See: http://belinfund.by/en/home/

24 SME Policy Index 2020 scores of 3.37 and 2.92 for Armenia and Georgia respectively, compared to regional average of 2.26.

25 https://seedblink.com/

26 See http://nelsongray.com/angels/business-angel-groups-networks/

27 See: http://fast.foundation/en/program/865

28 See: https://bana.am and https://aica.social

29 See: https://angelsband.by/en

30 See: http://uangel.com.ua/

31 See: https://www.businessangels.md/

32 See: https://www.eban.org

33 https://www.eif.org/what_we_do/equity/news/2013/pgff.htm

34 https://www.eif.org/what_we_do/resources/BIF2/index.htm

35 http://www.wbedif.eu/for-entrepreneurs/enterprise-innovation-fund-enif/

36 Vlerick Business School for Scale-Ups.eu. analysis of the European scale-up landscape using information collected on 80,451 scale-ups based in eight European countries – Denmark, Finland, France, Germany, Luxembourg, the Netherlands, Sweden and the UK; and a more fine-grained insight into the management practices of European scale-ups from survey data of 124 of scale-ups.

37 Azerbaijan has the highest rate of tertiary graduates in STEM relative to the size of the population aged 20-29 years in 2018 with over 56 male and 30 female graduates per thousand, followed by Belarus (47/19); Ukraine (29/12) and Georgia (15/10) (Eurostat, 2018, no data for Armenia and Moldova).

38 See for example: https://ec.europa.eu/regional_policy/en/projects/Poland/south-eastern-poland-sees-global-success-with-innovative-tech-talent-recruitment-platform

39 See: https://www.catalyst.am/

40 See: https://evconsulting.com/what-kind-of-skills-will-be-required-for-the-future-of-jobs-in-armenia/

41 https://www.businessfinland.fi/en/do-business-with-finland/startup-in-finland/startup-permit

42 The Estonian Start-up Visa was launched in January 2017 and aims to attract business founders from non-EU countries but also new talent to Estonian start-up and scale-ups.

43 https://startupvisalithuania.com/startup-visa-lithuania/benefits/

44 See: https://www.businessfinland.fi/en/do-business-with-finland/work-in-finland

45 See: https://www.businessfinland.fi/en/for-finnish-customers/services/programs/talent-boost-finland

46 The recipient companies in Estonia have the obligation to pay at least Estonia's average salary to the foreign specialists they hire.

47 See: https://www.zdnet.com/article/startup-powerhouse-why-estonia-needs-more-developers-tech-talent-in-jobs-boom/

48 https://e-resident.gov.ee/nomadvisa/

49 Digital nomads and remote workers have long faced ambiguity when working while they travel, often skirting around the law by working while visiting a country with a tourist visa.

50 This access is regulated via Deep and Comprehensive Free Trade Areas (DCFTA), part of each country's EU Association Agreement, which put in place a preferential trade system that allows the three countries to benefit from reduced or eliminated tariffs for its goods and an increase in access to services markets. Since the DCFTAs came into force, exports from the three countries to the EU have increased.

51 Ukraine is also making preparations for a so-called «industrial visa-free regime» allowing access for industrial products to the markets of Ukraine and EU countries on the basis of mutual recognition of the results of work on conformity assessment for industrial products

52 The EAEU includes Belarus, Kazakhstan, Russia, and Armenia. Armenia also maintains bilateral trade relations with the EU regulated by a Comprehensive and Enhanced Partnership Agreement (CEPA), provisionally applicable since June 2018

53 See: https://www.wto.org/english/thewto_e/whatis_e/tif_e/org6_e.htm

54 See: https://magazine.verdict.co.uk/verdict_magazine_may20/estonia_startup_ecosystem

55 See: https://gust.com/programs/virtual-bridge-accelerator

56 See: https://www.globalscot.com

Part III

A ROADMAP FOR BOOSTING THE POTENTIAL OF IHGES IN THE EESC

This handbook has examined the rationale for and the types of policy interventions that can be mobilized to support the creation, development and (international) growth of innovative high-growth enterprises. Based on the available evidence from a number of enterprise and innovation policy reviews, including on the UNECE Innovation Policy Index and Innovation for Sustainable Development Reviews of Belarus, Georgia and Moldova, the handbook has highlighted specific drivers and barriers for IHGEs in the EESC sub-region and has provided examples of existing public and/or private initiatives that seek to foster a positive environment for ambitious business ventures.

The six EESC countries are at a crossroads with each having certain promising 'green shoots' or clusters of transformative potential but at the same time, a number of regulatory, financial, geopolitical and 'knowledge' (education and research and innovation, etc.) infrastructure issues that limit the potential for the growth of transformative firms. A number of the factors influencing business growth potential are structural and the policy toolkit proposed in the handbook needs to be placed in the context of wider reforms. While we have sought to present examples from other (often more 'advanced') countries, the institutional structure and the state of governance (public and corporate) in the EESC countries may not always allow for the rapid and smooth adoption of 'best-in-class' methods to support IHGEs.

Box 3.1 Growth paths

The Cambridge Judge Business School has identified two decision dimensions that underpin a company's growth approach:

- First, whether a company seeks growth through the same offering (set of products, services and solutions) or whether it expands its offering;
- Second, whether a company seeks growth within the same industrial/market sector or whether it ventures into a new one.

The two dimensions indicate possible "growth paths" that may take a company from the current sector and offering to multiple sectors with a diverse set of offerings.

The Growth Paths Matrix

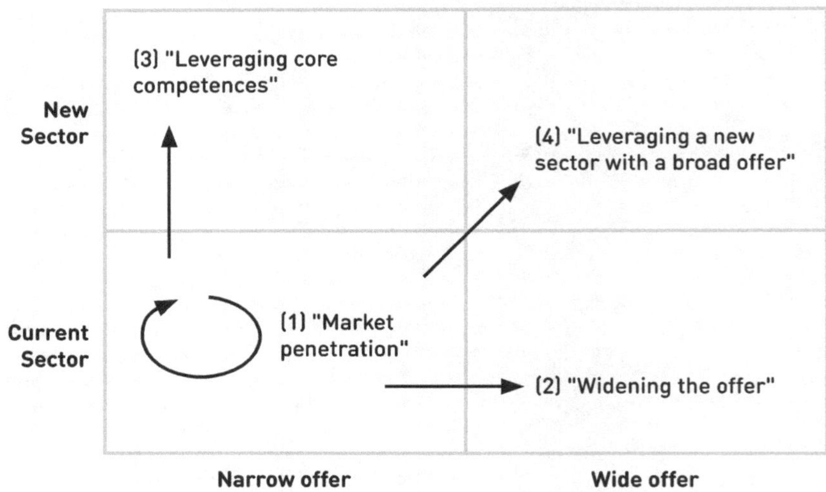

Source: UNECE, adapted from (Barclays, 2016).

Transformative change and new value generation driven by IHGEs requires the development of a **cross-cutting and holistic approach**. High-growth firms will not emerge as the result of a process that brings together piecemeal solutions; rather it requires a coordinated set of actions with a clear strategic objective applied at cross-government and multi-stakeholder levels.

The interviewees from the EESC sub-region, that provided detailed local knowledge for the handbook stressed the importance of **finding the most effective growth paths** rather than focusing only on a single model. At the level of an individual business, a growth path can take several directions as illustrated in Box 3.1.

From a policy perspective, **five main routes for fostering IHGEs** can be identified:

1. Support for the acceleration/scaling of (high-tech) start-ups;
2. Encouraging growth of established manufacturing or service firms through product development and market penetration;
3. Backing corporate spin-offs from large national or multinational firms;
4. Attracting ambitious entrepreneurs and/or scalable companies from abroad to establish locally and grow globally;
5. Bringing support for research-based spin-offs emerging from public research institutes or higher education institutions.

Table 3.1 Comparative relevance of policy intervention routes for IHGE

Country/ Route	Scaling start-ups	Growth companies	Corporate spin-offs	Attracting ambitious entrepreneurs	Research spin-offs
Armenia	established route	emerging route	emerging route	emerging route	emerging route
Azerbaijan	emerging route	under-used route	emerging route	under-used route	under-used route
Belarus	established route	under-used route	under-used route	emerging route	emerging route
Georgia	established route	emerging route	under-used route	emerging route	emerging route
Moldova	emerging route	under-used route	under-used route	under-used route	under-used route
Ukraine	established route	under-used route	emerging route	under-used route	under-used route

under-used route   emerging route   established route

Source: Author's analysis for UNECE.

The extent to which each of these routes are realistic for each country varies but the order above broadly reflects the current potential for applying each route in the EESC sub-region. The figure below builds on the findings of the interviews conducted with the EESC stakeholders in preparation of this handbook and summarizes the relevance of the identified five routes for the six EESC countries.

Currently, the main policy effort has been *focused on building "start-up ecosystems"* generally in the ICT field and more specifically in digital services and software but with some "hardware" elements linked to the Internet of Things, AI, and the like. A lot of effort by both public agencies and private stakeholders to foster start-up communities has been made but instruments such as **accelerators are still insufficiently developed** and the focus on the start-up phase rather than later scale-up phases remains problematic.

Some examples of initiatives for the "growth companies" route exist, notably linked to cluster policy and export development support but they are rarely targeted towards potential IHGEs and are more general business development service approaches. Georgia and Armenia seem to have the most developed policies for this route – however, this remains an under-exploited potential in the EESC sub-region partly due to **the 'broad-brush' approach to SME policy and the lack of expertise in public-sector enterprise agencies**.

The corporate spin-out route, including via open innovation type initiatives, has been explored in Ukraine (see Box 2.13), as well as via the established multinationals in ICT field in Armenia, and is viewed as a route in Azerbaijan concerning large state and multinational companies.

The "attracting ambitious entrepreneurs" route is being explored in Azerbaijan, notably via various 'high-tech or IT' park incentive systems but also via other tools such as m-residency. Overall, this route seems like a long-term objective as the high-growth ecosystem (investor, services for IHGEs, etc.) would need to be more attractive and better promoted and the legislative framework as well as exit possibilities for investors improved.

The research-based spin-offs route remains a more difficult route in all six countries, although there are examples of research spin-offs emerging through various start-up ecosystems. The difficulty with this route is linked to the structural underinvestment in public research systems and the immaturity of knowledge transfer and valorization structures in the six countries.

The remainder of this concluding section is structured in two parts:

- The necessary steps to establish a policy framework, policy management and implementation system for IHGEs.
- Cross-cutting recommendations and specific policy options for the six EESC countries.

3.1 Designing and implementing a policy for IHGEs

The distinction between SME, start-up and IHGE policies has been explained above. The policies are obviously interlinked and rather than viewing them as separate interventions, it is better to think of them as part of a single broader process of applying different policy levers to businesses based on their characteristics (growth stage) and by taking account of trigger points.

Figure 3.1 · From broad-based SME policy to a targeted focus on IHGE

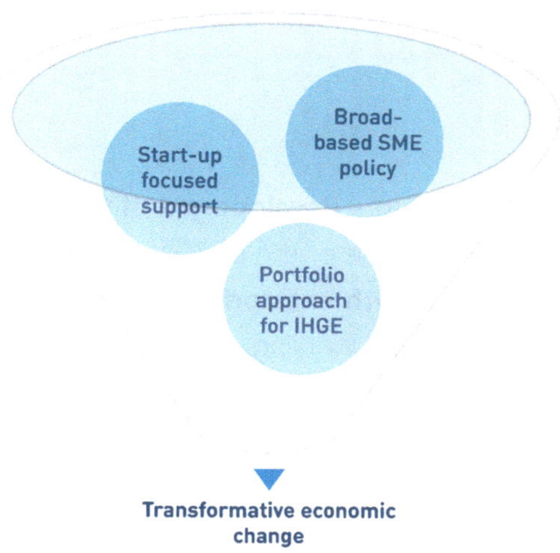

Source: UNECE

Such a targeted approach requires getting the institutions and processes right at both the overall strategic policy level and throughout the operational implementation which should be about **coordinating the support provided to IHGEs** from different public-private actors rather than just designing a 'programme' run by a ministry or agency.

To simplify, action is required at two main levels:

- *Policy making level:* a stronger and clearer set of priorities and a package of policy measures to optimize the potential for IHGEs;
- *Policy delivery level:* developing the capacity within the business support ecosystem to provide tailored support to IHGEs.

Policy design and strategic intelligence for IHGEs

At the current time, **none of the six EESC countries have a policy framework[1] that fosters the design and delivery of more targeted IHGE policies**. To help remedy this, six key steps are proposed for the development of a policy framework for IHGEs.

The six steps are aligned with a typical policy cycle process running from baseline analysis to evaluating the impact of the policy (and hence comparing with the baseline situation).

Figure 3.2 • Six steps for developing an IHGE policy

step 1	Development of an evidence base
step 2	Stakeholder task force on IHGEs
step 3	Government decision (policy priorities)
step 4	Action plan (cross-government/multi-annual)
step 5	Pilot IHGE programme
step 6	Evaluation of policy impact (after 3-5 years)

Source: UNECE.

The effort required for the first step – **development of the evidence base**, should not be underestimated as currently none of the EESC countries have in place comparable **statistics and data on high-growth enterprises** (e.g. in line with the Eurostat/OECD definition). National statistical offices working with the SME agencies should make this a priority (e.g. by twinning support from EU countries statistical offices). However, to enable the development of a client management system during implementation, the elaboration of better-quality official statistics is only a first step.

In addition, some EESC countries are **tracking start-up and scale-up businesses**, as is being done by the TechUkraine platform[2] which maps data on key tech players in the ecosystem, including workspaces. Such tools provide a basis for discussion and analysis of growth potential and should be extended beyond specific tech fields to better cover existing manufacturing and service companies with growth potential (e.g. by tracking increases in annual turnover, mergers or acquisitions that can indicate 'trigger points' of growth). Other platforms, such as the UK Scaleup Institute, also provide models for mapping and tracking (monitoring) over time the growth/scale-up ecosystem. The advantage of building such a platform is that it provides a means of monitoring enterprises' performance over time both for internal purposes and for the promotion of specific cases of 'high-growth champions' nationally.

To develop the policy framework will require **a dedicated governmental unit**. This does not necessarily mean recruiting additional staff (although it may be necessary to train existing staff or recruit one or more specialists, e.g. data analysts) – rather this is about bringing together a team of 3-5 people responsible for driving the policy development process forward. These people could be drawn from an SME agency or seconded from existing private initiatives supporting enterprises.

The **strategy design process** coordinated by a high-growth policy unit should be done in partnership with a stakeholder group of public-private actors involved in the support of or delivering services to businesses. This is where **a task force is established** as an important second step in the policy process. The task force's role is to propose a set of priority actions as an overall strategic framework for boosting the number and scale of IHGEs in the country.

The recommendations of the task force would be cross-departmental given the need to address both structural, institutional and legislative challenges (**getting the enabling environment right first**) as well as designing interventions that bring together and make available a 'portfolio' of support from different government or public-private sources. These recommendations would make up for the policy priorities and the third step in the policy process.

As a result, the **action plan** should be developed as the next step. It should cover a period of 4-6 years to allow the necessary time for testing and evaluating the proposed actions. Within the planned actions, a roll out of **a pilot IHGE programme** would be a critical next step. On a more detailed level, the OECD has proposed a timeline for a pilot programme in support of IHGEs in Belarus which is a relevant framework for reflection by Governments in all the EESC countries.

At the final stage of the policy process, the implementation of an IHGE action plan should be monitored by setting up transparent, accountable and flexible **mechanisms to implement and evaluate** the support measures.

Figure 3.3 • Suggested timeline for a pilot programme for high-growth enterprises

	Year 0	Year 1	Year 2-3	Year 4
Activities	**Assess firm's eligibility** • Motivation to participate • Growth potential • Social spillovers	**Review company's status** • Identify barriers to growth **Define growth plan** • Set strategic objectives • Link plan's activities to expected rules • Assessing funding sources	**Implementation of growth plan** • Develop workforce plan • Enhance managerial capacity • Adjust internal processess • Develop links between firm and knowledge institutes • Expand client base	**Evaluation of progress achieved** • Impact on firm's performance **Provide further financial assistance**
Tools	**Recent growth indicators** • Past growth rates • Organisational change • Increase in staff • Search of growth potential	**Business Diagnostics** • Firm's business diagnosis › Business concept › Organisation › Operations › Customer relations • Sector-specific diagnostics • SWOT analysis	**Capacity building** • Specialist/managers coaching • Core skills training/ workshops **Relational support** • Network of peers and mentors • Trade and foreign fairs **Financial assistance** • Matching grants to access BDS	**Assessment** • Company surveys, econometric studies **Provide further financial assistance** • Grants, e.g. for further R&D • Soft loans
Role of SME Agency	• Raise SME awareness about the programme • Analyse recent growth performance • Firms selection	• Perform initial business diagnostic • Identify external advisors to provide training/consulting • Provide financial support to SMEs (e.g. matching grants) • Monitor progress in programme implementation		• Carry ou impact assessment • Provide further financial assistance

Source: UNECE, adapted from (OECD, 2020).

Policy delivery level

At the operational level, the enterprise (SME) and/or innovation agencies in the EESC sub-region should develop a segmentation strategy that combines **'business demographic' indicators** for a first level segmentation with **qualitative criteria on 'trigger points' for growth** gathered through interaction between staff (e.g. client focused staff, export or enterprise programme managers, etc.) and potential or existing client firms.

An outline of a step-by-step process could be:

- Cross-referencing with data from the business register on additional company characteristics (e.g. changes in ownership or management);
- Cross-referencing with data on past support to understand the 'trajectory' of client companies and assess future additionality of support;
- Introducing a set of qualitative characteristics (trigger points, etc.) to enable a more strategic segmentation drawing on data compiled by the agency staff in a client management system;
- Further refining the segmentation process based on priority foreign markets, national sectoral/cluster or innovation (or smart specialization) priorities.

A "High-Growth Enterprise Unit" within an existing SME agency is more cost-effective and sustainable than creating a separate agency. An alternative would be to set up an inter-agency unit that would ensure an increased focus on relational support to the identified segments of potential IHGEs. Whichever path is ultimately chosen, it is critical to **design and build a support portfolio that reflects firms' life-cycles**, i.e. support options for each stage of growth that are mobilized in a timely manner.

This would include diagnostic assessments of potential IHGEs, identifying external advisers, bringing together networks of investors and scale-ups as well as running tailored growth programmes for cohorts of IHGEs (see examples from the policy toolkit section).

3.2 Cross-cutting recommendations: an EESC sub-region business scale-up initiative

The handbook has highlighted a range of existing initiatives in the EESC countries and presented several cases of policy interventions taken at both the national and multi-country level. The previous section has charted out a possible step-by-step process for developing a national level policy framework for IHGEs. However, as has been previously noted the institutional framework, the available experts and the investment communities of the six EESC countries are not yet sufficiently developed and would benefit from being part of a broader regional initiative which could be structured as presented below in Figure 3.4.

Figure 3.4 • A possible framework for an EESC sub-region IHGE facility

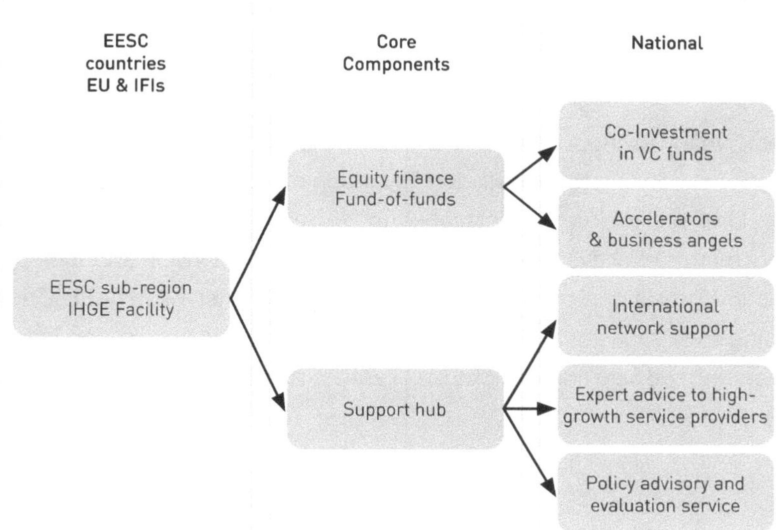

Source: Author's analysis for UNECE.

The WB EDIF programme in the Western Balkans is a relevant model for the EESC countries since it combines equity financing and support services for high-growth and innovative SMEs into a coherent package (in addition to a loan guarantee facility for SMEs). As was detailed earlier, the role of equity finance (equity crowdfunding, business angels, VC) in driving professional development of potential IHGEs is critical.

A **fund-of-funds operating at the sub-regional level** would provide a mechanism for investing in national co-investment funds (with business angels or VC investors) with a focus on supporting companies that would expand regionally and then globally. At the multi-country level, the possibility of developing an **EESC sub-region business angel network** to encourage cross-border investment could also be explored.

The support hub as part of such a facility would provide expertize to help adjust legal frameworks for investment, as a pre-condition for improving access to finance for IHGEs (including for equity crowdfunding and business angels) covering all stage of investment from seed and early stage to growth capital. The support hub would supply advisory services (technical assistance) to national SME agencies and related bodies on moving to a portfolio (client management) approach to support IHGEs or set up pilot IHGE programmes.

In the short-term, while such a facility is designed and launched, the opportunity to enhance regional co-operation in designing, implementing and monitoring policies for IHGEs should be pursued by preparatory work (e.g. improving statistical data on high growth enterprises, reviewing regulatory barriers to high-growth firms and so forth) at the national level and a regional EESC task force bringing together the main national stakeholders, international financial institutions, the OECD and EU programmes supporting the EESC countries

UNECE stands ready to support EESC countries in enabling IHGEs to take on a strong role in building and enhancing the foundation for sustainable development. As this handbook lays out, the EESC sub-region has substantial, underused potential for IHGEs. To enable and promote such firms effectively, EESC countries need the right vision and the appropriate policy tools and institutional capacities. UNECE is ready to further assist the EESC economies in developing their capacity to carry out efficient IHGE policy, building on its members` rich experience in the field and with the excellent assistance of the development partners.

Annexes

Table Annex 1 Commonly used definitions for high-growth enterprise

Definition	Source
High-growth enterprises are enterprises with average annualized growth in the number employees greater than 20 per cent per year, over a three-year period and with ten or more employees at the beginning of the observation period.	Eurostat-OECD Manual on business demography statistics (2008)
Gazelle enterprise: a **gazelle** is a high-growth enterprise that is up to 5 years old	Eurostat-OECD
High-impact companies are firms whose sales have at least doubled over a four-year period and which have an employment growth quantifier of two or more over the same period.	Spencer L. Tracy, *Accelerating Job Creation in America: The Promise of High Impact Companies*, Research report commissioned by the U.S. Small Business Administration, No. 381 (2011)
Growth Super Heroes are firms that have experienced growth in labour productivity in a 3-year period by increasing both turnover and employment and with labour productivity levels above the SIC 3- digit industrial average productivity level in the base year.	Jun Du and Karen Bonner, Fast-growth firms in the UK, Enterprise Research Centre, United Kingdom (2017)
High-growth SMEs (HGSMEs) are commercial firms with a cumulative sales increase of more than 50 per cent over three years.	SME Financing Data Initiative, Canada (2006)

Source: Author's analysis for UNECE.

Box Annex 1 Equity funding of IHGEs – two examples from Armenia

Case: Krisp
Product/service: AI powered speech enhancement
Number employees: 45

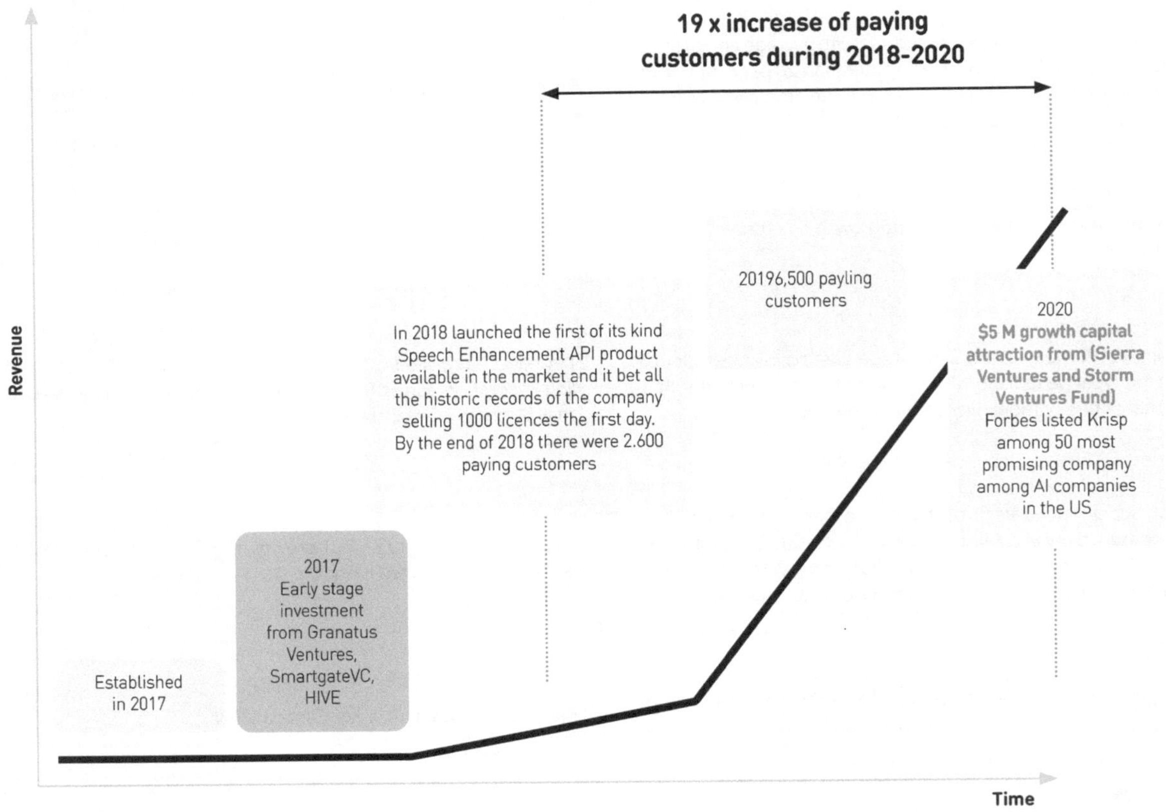

Source: EV Consulting / Granatus Ventures.

Box Annex 1 Equity funding of IHGEs – two examples from Armenia (Concluded)

Case: Menu.amp
Product/service: food delivery marketplace
Number employees: 239 excl. service contracts

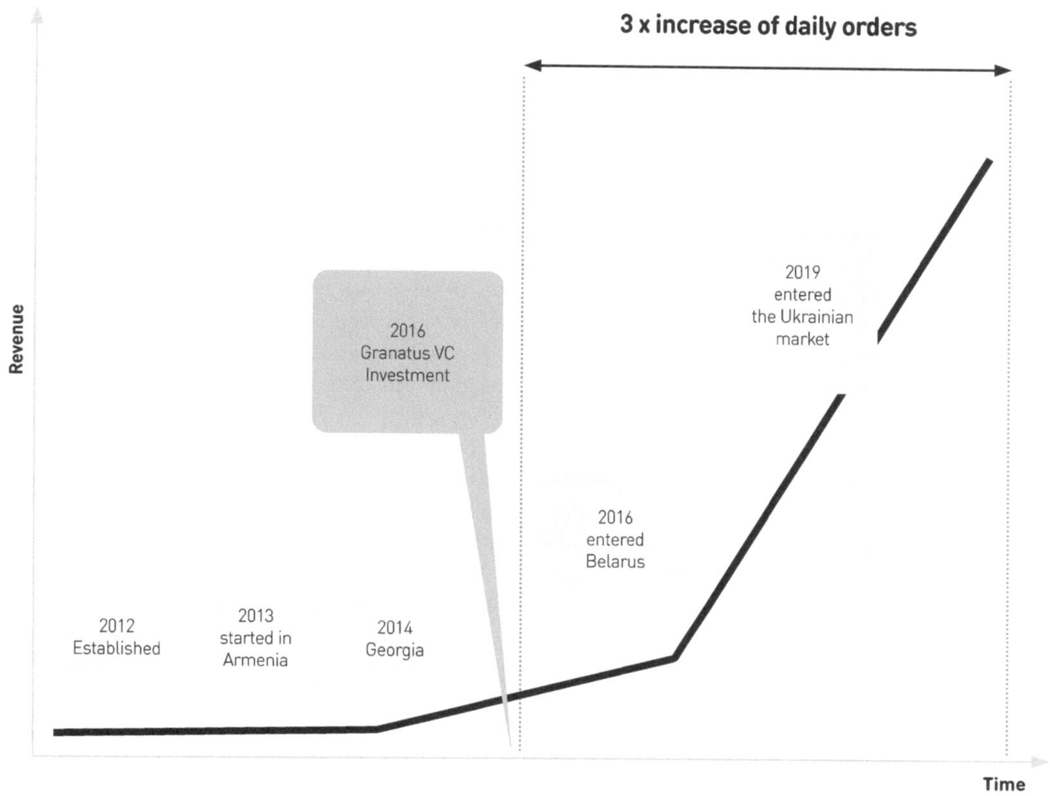

Source: EV Consulting / Granatus Ventures.

Box Annex 2 Developing STEM skills in the EESC sub-region: examples from Armenia and Ukraine

Building on the success of the **TUMO Centre for Creative Technologies**[a], which runs a unique learning programme made up of self-learning activities, workshops and project labs around 14 learning targets for teenagers, the EU TUMO Convergence Centre for Engineering and Applied Science, funded by the EU, will soon open its doors in Armenia. The centre will be a hub for research, education and start-ups, bringing together local and international partners to bridge the gap between higher education and industry in Armenia. The French University in Armenia is a major partner of the project.

The campus will include infrastructure for educational programming such as **TUMO Labs**, a STEM (science, technology, engineering, and mathematics) research laboratory, a conference centre and a revenue-generating commercial space to ensure the centre's long-term financial sustainability. TUMO Labs will constitute a logical continuation of the TUMO programme, allowing university students and young professionals to gain applied and state-of-the-art skills related to STEM subjects once they reach the age of 18.

A second initiative hosted at TUMO is **42 Yerevan**[b] which forms part of a global network leading completely free coding centres operating with the mission of providing highly-qualified specialists for Armenia's burgeoning programming industry. 42 Yerevan was founded in France in 2013 and its curriculum is based on the peer-to-peer model in which students tackle real-world problems, apply practical solutions to engaging projects and manage their own educational paths while working completely on their own. Using this method, over 95 per cent of the centre's graduates have gone on to find high-paying jobs in industry.

A number of initiatives exist in **Ukraine** on coding and other related skills required for the digital transition. For example, the **Kyiv Smart City Initiative**[c] was launched in 2018 in partnership with 10 city schools in different parts of the capital. Each school received the status of a partner in popularizing accessible IT education for children. Students will study Scratch, a programming language developed at the Massachusetts Institute of Technology to study the basics of coding, in school options. An Academy of Coding, created in partnership with the BrainBasket[d] Foundation, provides free classes that take place at Kyiv Smart City Hub. Young people work with professional tutors who have a strong practical background in best IT companies in Ukraine. More than 300 children have already participated in this educational course. Another example is the **Ucode IT-Academy**[e] located within the Unit.City innovation park. The education that takes place there helps to train IT-engineers and position them for jobs in leading IT companies.

Source: Author's analysis for UNECE.
[a] https://tumo.org
[b] https://42yerevan.am/
[c] https://www.kyivsmartcity.com
[d] https://brainbasket.org
[e] https://ucode.world/en/

Annex 3 List of the EESC stakeholders interviewed for the handbook

Name	Position
Anano Dolaberidze and Giorgi Chugoshvili	Founders of Phubber, Georgia
Andrii Komarovskyi	CEO of Sector X Accelerator Hub, Ukraine
Annie Vashakmadze	Head of Donor Relations and International Relations Department, Georgian Innovation and Technology Agency (GITA), Georgia
Bagrat Yengibaryan	Head of Enterprise Incubator Foundation, Armenia
Constantin Turcanu	Head of Analysis, Innovation and Entrepreneurial Training Department, Organisation for the Development of Small and Medium Sized Enterprises (ODIMM), Moldova
Dominique Piotet	CEO of UNIT.City, Ukraine
Emin Vali	Co-Founder of Keepface, Azerbaijan
Fidan Rustamova	Barama Innovation and Enterpreneurship Center, Azerbaijan
Hovik Musaelyan	Director of Synopsys Armenia
Igor Taranov	Head of the Expert Group on Innovation, Directorate for Science and Innovation, Ministry of Education and Science of Ukraine
Ihor Yegorov	Professor, Member of the National Scientific Council of Ukraine
Levan Chitadze and Giga Asanishvili	Founders of Sensor.ge, Georgia
Ludmila Antanovskaya,	Chairman of the Association of Advanced Instrument Manufacturers, Belarus
Manuk Hergnyan	Managing Partner of Granatus Ventures, Armenia
Mariam Kvitashvili	Deputy Head, Georgian Innovation and Technology Agency (GITA)
Natalia Dontu	Administrator, Moldova IT Park
Nikolay Shestak	Managing Partner, Zubr Capital, Belarus
Oleksandr Yurchak	President of the Association of Industrial Automation of Ukraine
Olha Krasovska	Senior SME Policy Advisor, FORBIZ project, Ukraine
Oxana Paladiciuc	Head of Division Business Support Infrastructure, Organisation for SME Sector Development (ODIMM), Moldova
Seymur Rasulov	CEO and Co-Founder of Whelp, Azerbaijan
Tural Kerimli	Chairman of the Board, İnnovation Agency Azerbaijan
Valentina Rakitina	Head of Ecosystem Department, UNIT.City, Ukraine
Vladimir Linev	Founder and Head of Adani, Belarus
Vusal Karimli	Managing Director of SUP Accelarator, Azerbaijan

Notes

1 For more details on the innovation policy framework and policy processes in EESC countries, please, see a UNECE "Sub-regional Innovation Policy Outlook 2020: Eastern Europe and the South Caucasus", 2021.

2 https://techukraine.org/ecosystem-map/

References

Arnold, E. F. (2014). *The case for public support for innovation. Department of Business, Innovation and Skills, UK.* Retrieved from https://www.gov.uk/government/publications/the-case-for-public-support-of-innovation-at-the-sector-technology-and-challenge-area-levels

Barclays. (2016). *Scale-up UK: Growing Businesses, Growing our Economy.* Retrieved from A report from the business schools at the University of Cambridge and the University of Oxford, convened by Barclays: https://home.barclays/content/dam/home-barclays/documents/who-we-are/our-strategy/Scale-up-UK-Growing-Businesses-Growing-our-Economy.pdf

BMWi. (2020). *Making space for innovation: the handbook for regulatory sandboxes.* Berlin: Federal Ministry for Economic Affairs and Energy (BMWi). Retrieved from Federal Ministry for Economic Affairs and Energy (BMWi), Germany: https://www.bmwi.de/Redaktion/EN/Publikationen/Digitale-Welt/handbook-regulatory-sandboxes.html

Brown, R., & Mawson, S. (2013). Trigger points and high-growth firms: A conceptualisation and review of public policy implications. *Journal of Small Business and Enterprise Development, 279-295.*

Calvino, F. C. (2016). *No Country for Young Firms?: Start-up Dynamics and National Policies.* Paris: OECD Publishing.

Cornelli, G. D. (2020). *Inside the regulatory sandbox: effects on fintech funding.* Retrieved from BIS: https://www.bis.org/publ/work901.htm

Echikson, W. G. (2020). *Europe's Collaborative Economy. Charting a constructive path forward.* Brussels: Centre for European Policy Studies.

EU SMEDA. (2017). *Sector Study of Precision Engineering in Armenia.* Retrieved from https://eu4business.am/uploads/20/09/01/36c2a8c27f2c9cc0adb0d02a541e41e9.pdf

EU SMEDA. (2019). *Tech & Entrepreneurial Ecosystem Mapping Report.* Retrieved from https://www.smeda.am/uploads/libraries/Tech%20and%20Entrepreneurial%20Ecosystem%20Mapping%20(web).pdf

European Commision. (2017). *Better Regulation Toolbox.* Brussels: European Commision.

European Commission . (2020). *Guidance from the European Commission on using the public procurement framework in the emergency situation related to the COVID-19 crisis.* Brussels: Official Journal of the European Union .

European Commission. (2014). *Public Procurement as a Driver of Innovation in SMEs and Public Services.* Brussels: European Union.

European Commission. (2015). *Fostering business angel activities in support of SME growth.* Brussels: European Union.

European Commission. (2015). *Policies in support of high-growth innovative enterprises . Part 1. Characterisation of innovative high-growth firms.* Retrieved from Publications Office of the European Union : https://op.europa.eu/en/publication-detail/-/publication/cb72538e-15af-40ed-aae2-1d35e2c7cd41

European Commission. (2019). *Annual report on European SMEs 2018/2019. Research & development and innovation by SMEs : background document.* Brussels: European Commission.

Flachenecker F., G. J. (2020). *High Growth Enterprises: demographics, finance and policy measures.* Luxembourg: Office of the European Union.

Grover Goswami, A. M., & Olafsen, E. (2019). *High-Growth Firms: Facts, Fiction, and Policy Options for Emerging Economies.* Washington DC: World Bank.

Hölzl, W. (2016). High Growth Firms in Europe. *Science, Research and Innovation performance of the EU,* pp. 247-276.

IRIS Group. (2019). *Nordic scalers - A study of drivers of growth and barriers to scaling of Nordic companies.* Retrieved from Nordic Innovation: https://www.nordicinnovation.org/2019/nordic-scalers-study-drivers-growth-and-barriers-scaling-nordic-companies

Isenberg, D. (2012). Focus entrepreneurship Policy on Scale, not Start-up. *Harvard Business Review.*

Lilischkis, S. (2011). *Lilischkis, S. (2011) Policies in support of high-growth innovative SMEs.* Brussels: European Commission, Directorate-General Enterprise and Industry.

Mason, C. (2013). Business angels. In L.-P. Dana, *World Encyclopaedia of Entrepreneurship* (p. 512). Cheltenham: Edward Elgar Publishing.

Mazzucato, M. (2015). *Building the Entrepreneurial State: A New Framework for Envisioning and Evaluating a Mission-Oriented Public Sector.* Levy Economics Institute of Bard College.

Mitchell, J. T. (2020). Tax incentives for R&D: supporting innovative scale-ups? *Research Evaluation,* 121–134.

Monteiro, G. (2019). High-growth firms and scale-ups: a review and research agenda. *RAUSP Management Journal,* 96-111.

NESTA. (2019). *Motivations to Scale. How European entrepreneurs think about growth and finance.* Retrieved from https://www.nesta.org.uk/report/motivations-to-scale/

OECD. (2010). *High-Growth Enterprises: What Governments Can Do to Make a Difference, OECD Studies on SMEs and Entrepreneurship.* Paris: OECD.

OECD. (2013). *An international benchmarking analysis of public Programmes for High-growth firms.* Paris : OECD Publishing .

OECD. (2016). *OECD Business and Finance Outlook 2016.* Paris: OECD Publishing .

OECD. (2018). *Promoting High-Growth Enterprises in ASEAN.* Paris: OECD.

OECD. (2020). *Monitoring Business Development Services and Supporting High Growth Enterprises in Belarus.* Paris: OECD Publishing.

OECD. (2020). *OECD Employment Outlook 2020: Worker Security and the COVID-19 Crisis.* Paris: OECD Publishing.

OECD. (2020). *Promoting Exports and Supply-Chain Linkages in the Food Industry in the Republic of Moldova.* Retrieved from www.oecd.org/eurasia/competitiveness-programme/eastern-partners/Promoting-Exports-and-Supply-Chain-Linkages-in-the-Food-Industry-in-the-Republic-of-Moldova-ENG.pdf

OECD. (2020). *SME Policy Index: Eastern Partner Countries 2020: Assessing the Implementation of the Small Business Act for Europe.* Paris/European Union : OECD.

OECD. (2018). Promoting High-Growth Enterprises in ASEAN. Paris: OECD.

OECD, EUROSTAT. (2018). *Oslo Manual 2018: Guidelines for Collecting, Reporting and Using Data on Innovation 4th Edition.* Paris/Luxembourg: OECD.

Parenti, R. (2020). *Regulatory Sandboxes and Innovation Hubs for FinTech.* Luxembourg: Policy Department for Economic, Scientific and Quality of Life Policies, European Parliament.

Peck, F. W. (2018). *Regulation and small business growth: Case studies from North West England.* London: Department for Business, Energy and Industrial Strategy, UK.

PWc. (2017). *Effectiveness of tax incentives for venture capital and business angels to foster the Investment of SMEs and start-ups.* Brussels: European Commission.

Ratinckx, E., & Raspoet, D. (2018). *High-growth innovative firms with impact.* Retrieved from Flemish Advisory Council for Innovation & Enterprise.: https://www.vlaamsindicatorenboek.be/nodes/72highgrowthinnovativefirmswithimpact/nl

Scottish Enterprise. (2018). *Scottish Enterprise Company Growth Support Case Studies.* Retrieved from Archives of the Scottish Parliament : https://archive2021.parliament.scot/S5_EconomyJobsFairWork/Inquiries/20180227-SE_Case_Studies.pdf

Segarra-Blasco, A., Teruel, M., & Jové-Llopis, E. (2018). High-growth firms in European countries: The role of innovation. *Revista Cuadernos de Economía, Universidad Nacional de Colombia -FCE*, 637-808.

Simonelli, F., & Renda, A. (2019). *Study Supporting the interim evaluation of the innovation principle.* Luxembourg: Publications Office of the European Union.

Tidd, J. B. (2005). *Managing Innovation: Integrating technological, market and organizational change. 3rd Edition.* Chichester, UK.

UNECE. (2020). *Sub-regional Innovation Policy Outlook 2020: Easstern Europe and the South Caucasus.* Geneva: United Nations Publications.

Upperquartile . (2013). *Evaluation of Scottish Enterprise Engagement with Account Managed Companies.* Retrieved from http://www.evaluationsonline.org.uk/evaluations/Search.do?ui=basic&action=show&id=530

Vlerick Business School. (2020). *European Scale-Up Report.* Retrieved from https://www.vlerick.com/en/research-and-faculty/knowledge-items/search/0/4/b/4/download-the-european-scale-up-report

Wilson, K. (2015). *Policy Lessons from Financing Innovative Firms.* Paris: OECD Publishing .

World Bank. (2019). *Path for Ukraine's Economic Growth : Technology Upgrading.* Retrieved from https://openknowledge.worldbank.org/handle/10986/32814

World Bank. (2020). *Realizing Armenia's High-Tech Potential.* Retrieved from https://openknowledge.worldbank.org/handle/10986/33027

World Economic Forum. (2019). *Global Competitiveness Report.* Retrieved from http://www3.weforum.org/docs/WEF_TheGlobalCompetitivenessReport2019.pdf

Zhao, M. D. (2019). *Characteristics of scale-ups and the impact of scale-up support programmes. A Literature Review.* Retrieved from The Evidence Network Inc. & 4FRONT OY for Nordic Innovation.: https://www.nordicinnovation.org/sites/default/files/inline-images/Literature%20review%202019-11-21.pdf